Tapping
into the crowd

How to create Competitive Advantage
from the Inside Out

An Coppens

AF271772

Published by PenCraft Books, LLC

PenCraft Books

Tapping into the crowd

For more information:
  www.gamificationnation.com
  @GamificationNat

ISBN: 978-1-939556-20-2 (Kindle)
ISBN: 978-1-939556-19-6 (Print)
ISBN: 978-1-939556-21-9 (PDF)

First published: January, 2017 USA

Published by: PenCraft Books LLC,
7348 Maple Terrace, Traverse City, MI 49686, USA

Acknowledgements

I am very grateful for the people that keep supporting me on putting a book together. It is always a leap of faith to go down the route of publishing your thoughts and ideas. I am hoping some of you will be inspired too.

My book has often had to take a back seat in and let business duties take front stage, during this both my editor Dawn Campbell and my publisher Barbara J Cormack from PenCraft Books were very patient as well as adding their expertise to the creation of the end result.

I also want to extend my gratitude to the fabulous cartoonist Nigel Sutherland, who captured the book and its chapters in great images.

I want to thank you as the reader for picking up the book and I hope you will be happy to share positive reviews and actions you have taken as a result with me online or in person.

Tapping into the crowd

Contents

INTRODUCTION

In my work, around of gamification design, I often get asked to create a process or embellish an existing process to stimulate employee engagement. For me most of the time employee engagement is closely aligned to company and management culture. It is no surprise that top rated companies in best companies to work for lists are there.

Typically, when people embark on using gamification for employee engagement, they are embarking on a digital transformation programme. Transformation being the real operative word, the digital part is more the enabler or method though which the change will take place.

What fascinates me and what drove me to write this book is that so many digital transformation companies don't start with the people. Gamification is often also called human centric design, which effectively puts the employee as the protagonist in the story. I truly believe the employee group is often an untapped resource. If you give them a platform and they feel their ideas are being valued, respected and implemented, then you unleash an exponential driving force, which most of your competitors will not be able to replicate.

Basically, what I am hoping to do with the book is to encourage leaders and managers to go a lot further into exploring how their own people can improve their team, environment, work practices, products, etc.

My wish is to inspire more people than I can reach in person through my writing and to see positive results and change happen on a global scale. This may sound even pretentious to some people, but I truly believe that most employees go to work to deliver a great day's work and do the best they can. Often they bump into stumbling blocks, in the shape of management, broken processes or non-fit for purpose technology. With technology as an enabler a lot can be achieved, but you have to mobilise the people first.

I hope that you will enjoy the book. I would also love to hear back from you what inspired you and when you have implemented something from the book and how it turned out.

Enjoy,
An

CHAPTER ONE
THE CROWD IS CHANGING
OUR BUSINESS LANDSCAPE

Tapping into the crowd

Unless you have been living under a rock this past decade, you can't help but notice, the majority of business related success stories are about tapping into the power of the crowd. Crowd sourcing and crowd funding have become very topical, in fact 85% of the best global brands have actively used this strategy in the past decade and its uptake is expected to grow. The crowd (people) has generated ideas throughout time, many of which result in innovations and inventions to solve problems – often even before we knew we had them.

Many business leaders and managers believe they need know everything and have a reluctance to hand over power to the crowd. In this book we want to explain how you could make crowd sourcing as an employee engagement strategy work to create sustainable competitive advantage.

The most familiar example of tapping into the crowd is probably social media; sites such as Facebook, Twitter, LinkedIn, Instagram, Pinterest etc. all of which rely on the crowd to generate the content. These sites provide the public with a platform, in-built teasers, and motivational game elements; all cleverly designed to keep us busy sharing, and more importantly, coming back for more.

Consider organisations like Uber, the taxi company, who don't actually own any taxis. They've asked people with cars to become their drivers and they've asked consumers to rank these drivers. This ensures a quality experience is achieved for all, with drivers rating consumers, and consumers rating their drivers. This model allows Uber to be a multi-locational organise, but with minimal start-up costs, plus their ranking system means they have reduced advertising costs because their geo-location software app helps two motivated parties find each other – quickly. This system also processes all bookings and payments, hence no cash changes hands.

Year on year, IT platforms are seeing an increase in crowd ranking and crowd voting techniques. Consequently, they have created solutions for technical problems like sifting through answers by ranking them according to relevance and applicability to the problem. A good example of this platform is Stack Overflow. They utilise the type of technology that enables the crowd to show them who is contributing valuable answers, sharing information, knowledge and skills. It goes as far as ranking questions, votes, and people on a leaderboard.

Crowdsourcing platform and marketing organisation eYeka, said in their 2015 trend report *The State of Crowdsourcing* "85% of the Best Brands of 2014 have used crowdsourcing over the past 10 years". With the FMCG (fast moving consumer goods) industry leading the pack, some other top users in this field include: Procter and Gamble, Unilever and Nestle.

In the graph below you will see which industries are actively engaging in this pro-active business technique. The majority have used it for content creation. Others use it for generating new ideas for their client facing approach. I use it to source valuable ideas to help me transform my brand, deliver innovation, and find out what else I could be doing to create a differentiator for my gamification business.

Tapping into the crowd

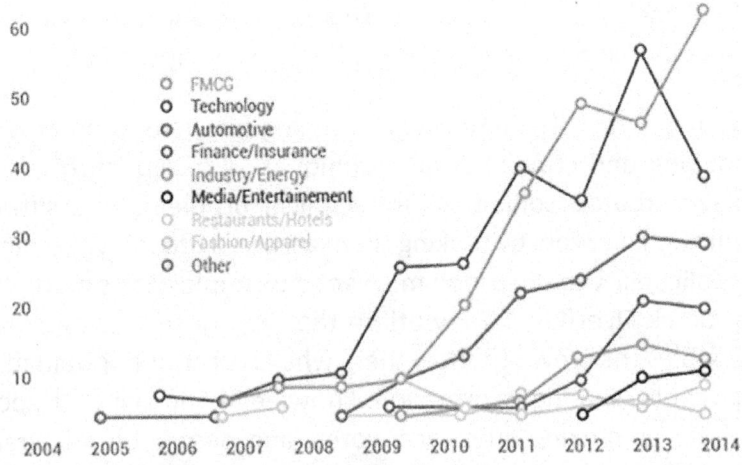

Figure 3: Evolution of crowdsourcing usage by the Best Global Brands, broken down by sector

(Graph source from eYeka State
of crowdsourcing report 2015)

It's probably not surprising to learn that the most frequently used method of crowdsourcing is video creation. This is mainly due to the popularity of video channels from the YouTube generation of bloggers. Idea crowdsourcing comes next, which I found surprising, considering hack-a-tons for innovation and organisational improvement have been around for nearly twenty years. Yet many organisations are still not tapping into their internal crowd, possibly due to a lack of know-how on how to engage the power of this source and a fear by management to be seen as not knowing everything or worse still to be undermined with new ideas and ways of working.

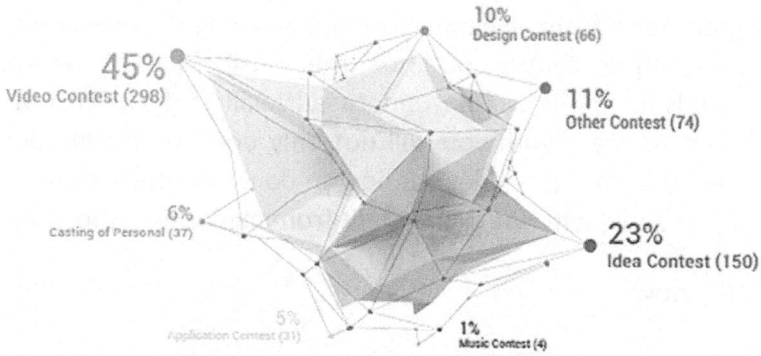

Figure 7: Type of content crowdsourced in the last decade by the Best Global Brands

Type	Usage by brands	Example
Video crowdsourcing	Authentic, consumer-based brand storytelling	Since 2006, Doritos has involved consumers in creating advertisements that would air during the Super Bowl.
Idea crowdsourcing	New product, service or concept creation	In 2014, Oral B launched the world's first connected toothbrush, inspired by ideas submitted to an eYeka contest.
Design crowdsourcing	Packaging and retail concept creation	In 2014, the Serbian brand Doncafé launched a redesign packaging, created by a contest winner from California.
Casting or Personal Stories	Featuring consumers in campaigns	In 2006, McDonald's "Global Casting Call" crowdsourced consumer stories and featured the best ones on its food packaging.
Application crowdsourcing	Find mobile, TV or augmented reality app ideas	In 2014, Ford launched a series of contests to create applications that improve mobility in some of the world's most challenging cities.
Music crowdsourcing	Allowing consumers to invent jingles to remix ringtones	In 2011, Nokia asked the Audiodraft community to give its iconic "Grand Valse" ringtone, which appeared in 1992, a crowdsourced lift.
"Others"	Variety photography, illustration, entrepreneurship or other contests	In 2013, the Thomson Reuters Foundation and Nokia invited photographers to submit images capturing many aspects of women's empowerment around the world.

Table 2: Types of creative crowdsourcing and examples.

(Graph and table source from eYeka State of crowdsourcing report 2015)

Tapping into the crowd

Operationally speaking; performance management and HR - the people centric part of the business – is where crowdsourcing is still an underused facility. So what I am about to share with you will not only open your mind and eyes to what is possible, but how to do it, and perhaps more importantly, why you will benefit from exploring it too.

Why now?

Since the early 2000s, thanks to the emergence of social media, crowd sharing, which includes on-line communication, has become the norm. Social media enables us all to amplify our messages. Consequently, we have grown used to the techniques necessary for tapping into the crowd. What these platforms have done is to give the ordinary person a voice. This enables people to share whatever they want to share, whenever they want, to the point it drives and influence opinions. It has become an incredibly powerful network.

Most CEOs admit to wondering how to tap into the crowdsource when actually, they already have their own internal crowdsource – their employees. Added to which, many senior executives are shielded from their employees by middle management, so lack a real understanding of what is truly being experienced within their business. Hence the global popularity of TV shows like *Undercover Boss,* whereby a boss goes undercover to gain first-hand experience, what it's like to be an employee.

Many CEOs I speak to, in both my executive coaching career and currently in my gamification business tell me they're doing their best, but they're often not convinced if their decisions are right for customers, employees, and the business. This is based on the fact they are overloaded with data coming at them from all angles.

The volume of data that we're all now able to capture is infinite; for some it's become a relentless assault on their senses. Consequently, a lot of executives admit, albeit it privately, that being responsible for making the right decisions, at the right time, is getting progressively harder to achieve and they sometimes feel like they are 'winging it'. Therefore, they cannot be 100% sure of their next action, or whether their strategy is even going to hit the right target.

A Harvard Business School study listed the top 5 fears of 116 CEOs of Fortune 500 companies:

1. Being seen as incompetent.
2. Underachieving.
3. Being too vulnerable.
4. Being attacked politically by colleagues.
5. Appearing foolish.

These fears resulted in a variety of dysfunctional behaviours such as:

*   A lack of honestly in their communications.
*   Too much political game playing.
*   Silo thinking.
*   A lack of ownership and or follow-through.
*   Tolerating bad behaviours.

That is a tough place for anyone to be in, never more so than for a leader. Subsequently, many CEOs say they feel isolated; they worry about getting it wrong, and they worry that people will discover they're a fraud because they *don't* actually know *everything*. Of course no-one does, that's why it's important to admit when we don't know something. It is not a sign of weakness, rather a strength to admit what we don't know, then outsource or hire the relevant expertise required. I don't know everything in my business; there will always be knowledge gaps, issues I don't know how to solve, so I know I need other people to step in and fix them for me.

Disruptive companies have experienced this, so they're tapping into the crowd to provide them with instant feedback. It is this *instant* feedback loop that makes social media so popular. Who doesn't like to receive a *like*? Who doesn't like it when their information is worthy of being *shared*? Consequently, feedback has become a valuable tool for building both personal and organisational reputations.

Just because you are the CEO, director, or manager of an organisation doesn't mean that employees are going to like or even value everything you say. Nevertheless, they're still invested in whatever you have to say because they want to get paid. However, *when* you ask them to collaborate with you, and plan the best way forward, or create a strategy that will solve an issue, *then* you're more likely to receive a positive response that could provide you with a totally different perspective.

A parcel delivery service manager was aware that their website needed some attention to improve the customer experience. I.T. based work was normally outsourced to external experts. However, this time the CEO asked his internal crowd "How they could improve the web experience for customers"? Over a period of one month, ideas were accepted and voted by employees, prizes were awarded for implemented ideas. Consequently, the CEO received 40% more ideas than normally received from external sources. Plus, they saved 70% in comparative consulting fees, after deducting the cost of prizes and time spent evaluating ideas.

Crowd engagement is extremely powerful in creating competitive advantage. Imagine what could happen when you tap into the in-house resource that is already available to you. Now imagine how accessing, and more importantly, utilising all that human intelligence and talent will influence your decision making. Tapping into employee intelligence allows you to create a multiplier effect; it's exponential - when used well.

Google is a company where they have worked out how to allow new idea generation to become an exponential source of ideas. Employees are allowed to pitch their ideas to spend a proportion of their working time on an innovative project of their creation. Some of these innovations have gone on to become actual additional services or features of Alphabet aka Google.

Disruption can be started from the inside out; the crowdsource techniques used by for example Uber, which assisted them in disrupting a whole industry and by creating a new business model, can also apply to your line of business and create competitive advantage. I challenge you to think, act and be different to other organisations in your industry. I dare you to take advice from your employees to make improvements from the inside out.

In many organisations, management and leadership are *still* all about setting vision, direction and keeping control. However, in our new world of work, there has been a shift towards employees becoming more involved. By being given more information, employees are able to positively influence a company's vision and direction - something I actively encourage. For example, if you want employees to rank and vote on the vision and direction, they need information to make educated, better informed decisions. I would go a step further, and ask employees to generate ideas about where the company could be heading, then select the best, or let employees vote.   When an employee's suggestion is championed, the *buy-in* generated has way more impact; it creates a sense of ownership, which simply is not there when you impose ideas onto others.   Creating a *buy-in* attitude, based on mutual understanding and acceptance, means employees know they are part of the decision making process, which is a strong ace to play in the game of business.

The modern employee has evolved; the millennials, and even generation X to a large extent grew up with all the latest social technology. They have grown to like and expect instant feedback.   They also like to have access to the decision makers. Additionally, they like to be in control, or at least to have some sense of being able to directly influence their environment. I think when you give employees the freedom and the resources to deliver what constitutes a great day's work they tend to achieve that. Not least because people by nature are willing to please. Of course there's bound to be a small percentage of people who hate going to work and who go with the purpose of delivering a bad day's work. However, most of us know that we need to provide an element of value in order to receive some element of reward (pay). When asked which would you rather deliver: *a fair day's work for a fair day's pay*, or a bad day's work, most of us have enough pride to opt for the former.

Every individual has talents.   Consequently, people are usually willing, when encouraged, to activate their particular talent; it's something they tend to enjoy doing. For instance,

I love designing; I'm a naturally creative person, so I'm always conceiving something new. To succeed in my field, I'm willing to give my greatest work - every day of the week. That's what drives me, it's my motivation. Most people are the same in that respect; they all have something they excel at, something that comes naturally to them, something that motivates them.

To find out what that special motivation is for each of your employees, you'll need to make a connection with them. Ask open questions like 'What do you love doing on a personal level that you would do automatically, even without payment'? They'll probably have a hobby they are passionate about, especially if it's not something already being fulfilled by their work. Some people have figured out what their passion is and are actually working in the field they love. For instance, I know some sales people who love communicating; so they love selling, they love the thrill of negotiating a deal. They wouldn't like to do anything else, and even in their spare time, that's what they do, they sell ideas, they sell themselves at parties and any occasion they can because they are natural born networkers - they never switch off.

Find the people in your organisation that are already living their passions, enable them to be their best, and you'll find they'll reward you with their best. It's not an easy thing for a CEO to find the time to make such drastic changes, but it is a rewarding thing to do. If you're in any doubt about the rewards, I recommend reading *Reality is Broken* by Jane McGonigal. It provides us with a young person's perspective of what it's like to go to work today, meaning, they've probably spent more time gaming of some kind than they've ever spent studying, or even working.

Tapping into the crowd

Today the vast majority of society engages in games: be they sports, or card and board games, or video and computer games, often on hand held devices. The reason why they turn to games is because they want that instant gratification, that little figurine that jumps up and down shouting "Hey! Job well done. You made it to level 365". This gives us a sense of achievement, of actually doing something right, of getting better at something. We know what we need to do to level up, it's often repetitive, but it's providing us with instant feedback about how we're doing. It's creates the motivation to solve a challenge. It is what people are voluntarily opting in to compete and complete.

A work challenge can be equally rewarding, but for most of us in the workplace, we only get feedback through an annual or bi-annual review, which is far removed from the instant feedback that motivates us. Only customer facing professions receive more instant feedback if they are observant. Consequently, traditional performance appraisal systems are dying; they're no longer a good fit for motivating the modern employee. In fact, the old structure and frequency has lost its appeal and purpose for manager and employee alike. Appraisals are now jokingly referred to as having had the 'talk'.

Do we still need feedback? Yes, we do! Do we need to have an element of information flowing back and forth regarding career, goals and development? Absolutely yes we do! Neither the current nor the younger generation would disagree with that. They actually say *'Yes please'* to more feedback. They want to know what it takes to level up. They want to know, sooner rather than later, whether they will be considered for that next level. They also want to know what you will put on the line to help them achieve that next level, because this gaming generation expects more feedback, expects more access to you, and expects you to give them the resources to deliver.

Consider the amazing work done by WorldBlu, an organisation with a purpose of developing freedom-centred organisations and leaders. Their vision is to see one billion people lead and work in freedom. They have captured a way of doing business that is coming from the crowd, or from the inside out, and its core value is based on freedom. They find that it creates optimal conditions for individual potential and collaborative success.

Another highly documented example is the Semco organisation and the work of Ricardo Semler in Brazil. Semco was a traditional, hierarchical organisation in the 1950s. They made money, but they were reaching a point where they were becoming a cost intensive and not so profitable organisation. What the younger son of the original owner said was "Okay. Let's try and organise this work space differently", which he did with drastic consequences, when his father passed the company over to him. He didn't tackle the whole organisation at once though. He started with small units and basically gave away the power to the people. He was considered crazy in his day. Today it's probably still considered a challenging and radical business approach.

In fact, when I was studying for my MBA while working for one of the leading management consultancy companies at the time, I was reading the book *Maverick* about Semco, so I learnt what they did to succeed. Ricardo Semler's *TED Talk* is equally entertaining and educational.

When I shared my views about the courage of Ricardo Semler

with one of the company partners, I said "Wow, this is amazing! We need to do more of this", the reply was "We've tried this, it's old school, and no it doesn't work for companies like ours". Naturally, I was surprised, I was quite curious as to where he had actually tried this and seen it fail to dismiss it so readily. I was in my late 20s at the time and the principles of *Maverick* never left me. I have always challenged myself to find a better way to make things happen, not least because there's more than a singular scenario that works.

What I found in the subsequent years of researching and following Semco is that they became a multi-million-dollar company. That's despite all the *naysayers* and the horrendous criticism Ricardo Semler got at the time. Effectively, he eroded the traditional hierarchal system and gave employees, of each operational team, the information they needed to make decisions. He also asked them to select the best person to lead specific projects, not unlike the TV show *The Apprentice,* where people pitch to be leader of a project, and the team chooses who they think will lead them to success.

Additionally, they were also able to choose their own salaries because they had access to the company finances, so they had realistic information on which to base these budgetary decisions. They also knew the industry benchmarks for different seniority levels, so they were given all the information they needed to make rational decisions. Furthermore, the teams were given the authority to prioritise the workload for each year. Essentially, the whole workload and management of the process, down to the last detail, was now being decided by the workers.

Obviously this philosophy won't suit every environment, culture or employee, but given the opportunity, the majority of people at Semco wanted to give it a good go. Consequently, it's this philosophy that has been credited with making the business successful again.

So I'd like to see more businesses adopting this kind of philosophy now. I think the time is right to embrace this kind of change, hence I believe this philosophy is an effective way forward. If you look at where disruption is happening, and where extreme success is generated, it's typically happening because of tapping into the power of the crowd.

I challenge all CEOs, VPs HR directors, operational managers and other decision makers to examine which areas of the business are you currently letting the power go untapped? Also, what could you potentially achieve when you choose to tap into it this power source?

This challenge may seem scary, and it will certainly take an element of courage to implement, nevertheless, I challenge you to consider how different is it from the scary place you're in right now where you have full accountability and total responsibility, and everything is resting on your shoulders?

How much easier would that burden be if some of the power, some of the responsibilities, and some of the decision making where shared?

All you have to do to lessen the burden is start tapping into the hidden power that is already available within your own workforce. Accepted, this is not necessarily a natural thing to do. Especially when you consider we live in an age where one of our economic values stem from the saying "Money is power", and a key measurement of a person's success, fame and fortune is determined by their financial status.

But, when you think about why you go to work, what's your answer? Is it for the money? I doubt it. In fact, 90% of people surveyed concur while money is a necessity, they don't actually go to work just for the money. Of course the money helps, so let's assume you already earn enough to be comfortable; what then is the real reason why you still go to work every single day? For most people it's the thrill of starting something, having a creative outlet, because they enjoy the social interaction; they hope to make a difference and fulfil a sense of purpose, or contribute to something bigger than themselves.

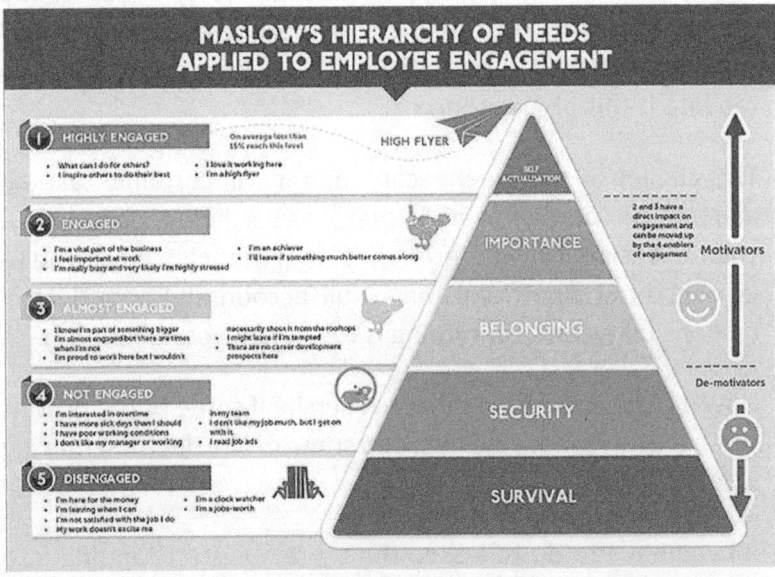

The reasons why most people work are as different as the people that are working. In many cases, when you repeatedly ask the question 'Why do you work'? (three or more times is the norm), you'll start to uncover the real reason, and the initial money answer becomes less valid. Why three or more times? Because it's a good rule of thumb; take a lesson from any child who intuitively knows that by repeatedly asking the same why question they'll quickly get the answer they want. For those of you with experience of children, you'll know exactly what I'm talking about. Often our first answer is the most obvious, also the most socially acceptable one. However, the second one is usually a bit closer to reality, with the third one and beyond getting nearer to the truth.

Oddly enough, the majority of people never question why they even go to work. Their automatic answer tends to be along the lines of 'it's just what people do to survive'. It's an answer that fills me with sadness because life is about thriving!

As this chapter concludes, you'll have answered some thought provoking questions that will prompt more self-reflection, all of which puts you in a stronger position to understand how a new way of thinking will positively impact on your workforce too.

Tapping into the crowd

References:
- Global crowdsourcing stats: http://eyeka.pr.co/99215-eyeka-releases-the-state-of-crowdsourcing-in-2015-trend-report
- http://www.crowdsourcing.org/editorial/global-crowdfunding-market-to-reach-344b-in-2015-predicts-massolutions-2015cf-industry-report/45376
- https://hbr.org/2015/02/what-ceos-are-afraid-of
- Book Reality is broken – Jane McGonigal Ted Talk of Jane https://www.ted.com/talks/jane_mcgonigal_gaming_can_make_a_better_world?utm_source=tedcomshare&utm_medium=email&utm_campaign=tedspread
- https://www.worldblu.com
- Traci Fenton talking about WorldBlu https://youtu.be/lHmRBgvmMpl
- Book Maverick – Ricardo Semler
- Ted talk of Ricardo https://www.ted.com/talks/ricardo_semler_radical_wisdom_for_a_company_a_school_a_life?language=en&utm_source=tedcomshare&utm_medium=email&utm_campaign=tedspread
- Maslow and employee engagement http://www.loyaltyworks.com/news-and-views/uncategorized/maslows-hierarchy-of-needs-and-employee-engagement/

5 P's OF THE
CROWD ECONOMY

BROUGHT TO YOU BY CSW³ & CROWDSOURCING WEEK

 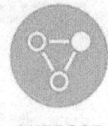   

PEOPLE	PURPOSE	PARTICIPATION	PLATFORM	PRODUCTIVITY
Empowering, disruptive, and human-centric	Creates meaningful experiences	Emphasis on co-creation and shared value	Medium to interact and drive results	Faster, cheaper, more efficient processes

CHAPTER TWO
EMPLOYEE ENGAGEMENT
AT CRISIS POINT

Tapping into the crowd

The Gallup Corporation say "Employee engagement is at an old time low globally" and they should know; they've been researching their global workplace audit since 2000.

- Last year they found that as few as 13% of employees were positively engaged in the workplace.
- In the US, that number is 32%.
- In the UK, it is around 20%.

This means that even though the majority of people, given the chance, would prefer to be in a position to work on something they believe in and deliver a good day's work, they aren't for a number of reasons.

Sadly, a vast number of people are going to work on autopilot, going through the motions, as if they were robots; basically, just doing the bare minimum to get paid, so they can go home again.

Finally, there is the remaining percentage of people, maybe 10% - 15% percent, who depending on the economy or company they are employed in, actively and passionately hate going into work.

Gallup's workplace audit focused on the following 12 employee questions, which are interesting questions for employers to understand in terms of a) where these feelings come from and b) how can managers and leaders influence these in a positive direction.

1. Do I know what is expected of me at work?

2. Do I have the materials and equipment I need to do my work right?

3. At work, do I have the opportunity to do what I do best, every day?

4. In the last seven days, have I received recognition or praise for doing good work?

5. Does my supervisor, or someone at work, seem to care about me as a person?

6. Is there someone at work who encourages my development?

7. At work, do my opinions seem to count?

8. Does the mission/purpose of my company make me feel my job is important?

9. Are my co-workers committed to doing quality work?

10. Do I have a best friend at work?

11. In the last six months, has someone at work talked to me about my progress?

12. This last year, have I had opportunities at work to learn and grow?

None of these questions are shockingly difficult, or shockingly crazy, so one wonders why so many organisations cannot provide environments whereby these questions could be answered more positively. Most companies, even ones that are registered on *best places to work* lists, have results that are not actually as good as one would expect to find.

We live in modern societies, where we think we have a lot of freedom and companies do their best to put in leadership training programs, support for managers, support for employees. Not so, hence employers are still experiencing the same old challenging issues that arise from employing a workforce that feels undervalued, unsatisfied, and is unlikely fully engage in the workplace.

Going back to the Gallup survey, when you consider the impact those 12 questions have on productivity, turnover, profit, and ultimately the customers, the results have an important net effect on a business' bottom line.

- When employees are clear about what's expected of them, and they have enough of the right materials and equipment to do a good job, productivity and turnover are increased; it also increases profit, and ultimately increases and strengthens customer relationships.
- When employees have an opportunity to express themselves they're more likely to deliver their best work, so again turnover, profit and customer relations go up.

Ultimately this is what most CEOs and what most senior executives want for their company. However, the fact is, some of these basics are often still lacking, so one could argue that perception and reality often differ. Even then, I would still say there is a case to be made to evaluate perceptions and look at what actions can be taken to remedy the situation (Oh and that doesn't necessarily mean making a big investment).

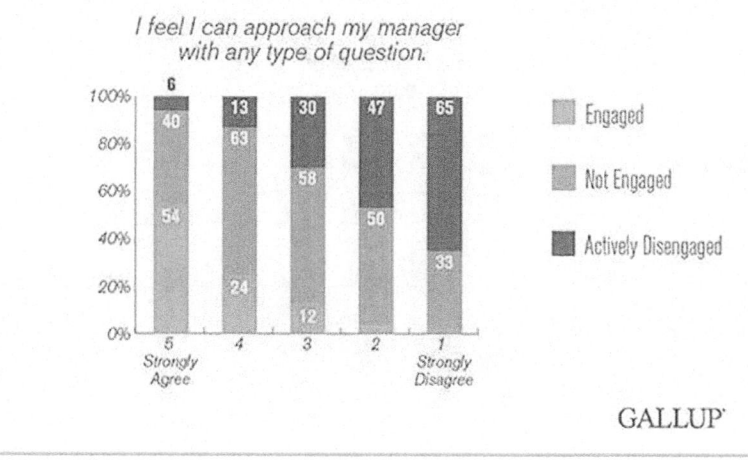

EMPLOYEES WHOSE MANAGERS ARE OPEN AND APPROACHABLE ARE MORE ENGAGED

A productive workplace is one in which employees feel safe enough to experiment, challenge, share information and support one another. The best managers get to know their employees and help them feel comfortable talking about any subject, whether it is work related or not. Among employees who strongly agree that they can approach their manager with any type of question, 54% are engaged. When employees strongly disagree, only 2% are engaged, while 65% are actively disengaged.

I feel I can approach my manager with any type of question.

GALLUP·

✓　When employee efforts are recognised and praised; productivity, profit, and customer relations go up.

✓　When an employee knows that their manager cares; again productivity, turnover, profit, and customer relations go up.

So, there is a lot a line manager can do to positively influence an employee's working life in an organisation. So much so, that since measurements began and details for leaving were recorded a whopping 60% were attributed to their line managers as the main contributing factor why an employee left their employment.

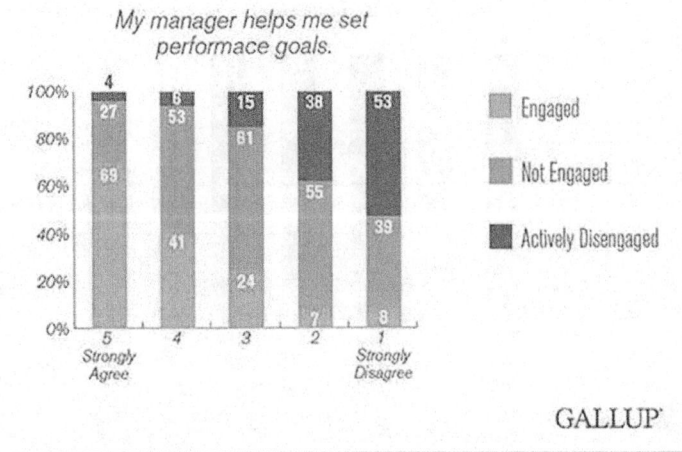

EMPLOYEES WHOSE MANAGERS HELP THEM SET PERFORMANCE GOALS ARE MORE ENGAGED

Engaged employees are more likely than their colleagues to say their manager helps them set performance goals and holds them accountable for their performance. To engaged employees, *accountability* means that their manager treats all employees fairly and holds everyone to the same standards, allowing those with superior performance to shine. Among employees who strongly agree that their manager helps them set performance goals, 69% are engaged. When employees strongly disagree, just 8% are engaged, while 53% are actively disengaged.

My manager helps me set performace goals.

Engaged
Not Engaged
Actively Disengaged

GALLUP

✓ When employees have development opportunities, productivity and profit are positively impacted.

✓ When employee's opinions are listened to, productivity and profit are positively influenced.

✓ When a corporate mission is clear, productivity and profit goes up.

✓ When there is a commitment to quality from everyone in the team from the top down, productivity and profit are positively impacted.

✓ When someone has a best friend at work, both productivity and customer relations are up, which means profit too.

✓ When employees feel that they have an opportunity to progress their role, or someone discusses progress on a regular basis, productivity and customer relations go up.

✓ When there are opportunities to learn and grow, these also positively impact on profitability.

When I read these findings, I find it puzzling that employers don't do more to look after their employees, added to which, these elements can easily be influenced, without having to invest in major ways. Some could even be rectified simply by creating and opening up channels of communication.

Research organisation Nielson did a study with young fast growing companies versus more traditional larger companies. Still using Gallup's 12 questions, they found a small difference in how things were perceived. However, the high growth, high performing companies and teams had more positive employee perceptions in response to all 12 questions compared to companies that were in declined or static. They also applied this strategy within departments and even smaller teams within organisation with similar results.

Findings generally proved that for those companies and departments that were able to sustain profit over a 10-year period, had remarkably different responses. Unsurprisingly, in those where profit declined or had become static, employees experienced less positive scores in all 12 questions. The biggest differences were having a sense of purpose; knowing why they were coming to work and knowing what they were supposed to do, they understood the expectations of what they needed to deliver.

Other key differentiators in making a difference to a

company's profitability were factors such as all employees being committed to quality and having the ability to display their best talents. So it makes sense to give leaders in organisation the ability to positively influence all of these factors and to provide structures that make their employees and teams happier.

When I look at today's strategic business models, very few of them actually use their employees as a core competitive advantage for driving their business forward. Most models that help you to decide on strategic objectives look outwards to the market, outwards to your competitors. Only on rare occasions do strategic models ever seem to positively engage with customers and even more rarely do they consider the opinions of an employee when it comes to setting up an organisation for success. Personally, I believe this is a tremendous oversight.

In a project I worked with for a multinational corporation, where in each of their 32 offices, CEO's had relative freedom to set the strategy for their country. The main proviso was that they each had to achieve the targeted numbers they promised to achieve based on projections and estimated business.

One forward thinking CEO approached me and said "I want my teams to be living and breathing our new strategy as well as letting them shape it to suit our unique business environment". He also advised me, that whilst the strategy design had already taken quite an evolved conceptual shape, there was a need and scope to translate this into something tangible. I worked closely with him on the communication exercise that was to promote the new vision, and deliver the necessary output from the various teams.

I asked him "Are you willing to give up control and to really let the people in your team decide how they implement your vision"? He said "Yes, obviously we need to provide some guidance and boundaries", to which I completely agreed and full heartedly supported. He went on to say "Ultimately, if the people can't deliver what we set out to do, then obviously we're missing the point somewhere". In my view it took courage for this CEO to take this kind of action, it also showed he trusted his people to come up with the right things at the right time. He did say he had some anxiety and nerves about letting go, but we made sure that any potential big risks were discussed and mitigated beforehand.

Not many managers are willing to actually give up that sense of control, and it's that sense of control that is killing a lot of the potentially positive answers that could come from the 12 questions in the Gallup employee survey.

When we look at global employee retention versus the statistics for people leaving organisations; typically, we find 40-60% of people leave their company because of their immediate manager. Research organisation Gallup said that managers or changes in management accounted for up to 70% of the variation in engagement statistics in their 12 question survey.

I challenge you to reflect on how much you support your people in setting expectations and letting them work to their strengths and talents. Do you give praise and recognition when they do a great job? Is the whole team working together towards a common goal, giving them the freedom and tools to deliver their best possible work? Do you know your team on a professional and also personal level based on regular interactions?

Of course it takes time to practice and develop these softer people skills, but it is what good leaders do, all leadership books ask you to be that kind of leader today.

Leaders that rise to the challenge and change are by definition becoming less command and control based. They know their new roles are more about influencing and supporting their teams towards a successful outcome.

If you truly want to work in a united organisation, where people are the power, and people are actually allowed to give their best work in return for fair pay and conditions, then it means the role of the leader and manager has got to change to one of being the motivator, an encourager, someone who reminds everyone about the corporate vision and mission, and makes sure that the team dynamics are working out. I see this management role becoming more like the conductor of an orchestra as opposed to some of the autocratic structures with hierarchical leadership types that are prevalent in many organisations, and may still be for years to come, if they don't change with the times.

So, the new leader of today and the future is much more of an encourager, a motivator, somebody who still has a firm grasp on what's important at all levels, but is capable of nurturing through meaningful praise while keeping people focused and on track. So, they'll be great communicators, meaning they will also be great listeners. Typically speaking, a lot of these skills have always been associated with women and feminine roles. I think we're seeing women and feminine qualities in particular becoming more prevalent, especially when defining more feminine structured leadership styles. By that I mean it is less about gender and more about feminine and masculine ways of leading. I have worked for some great men who displayed these qualities, and they challenged me to rise to the next level because I wanted to give my best possible effort. What I'm saying is we want to give everyone these chances to rise to their best possible version of themselves too.

With my leadership hat on, in the game context and with my gamification background, I too want to go down this route of offering strong encouragement, starting with challenging you to explore how games can motivate and develop your teams to do better. If you don't currently play any games, which I doubt given the variety available at this stage, just think sports, cards, board games, video games, computers, mobile games, etc. you'll realise just how prevalent games are to humans. But in case you really don't have any personal experience of games, just ask a teenager to show you the game they're playing. Ask them how it works, and how it tells them whether they're doing well or not, and then how they plan to level up.

Typically, the answer will be that it's the heads up display (HUD) which are the numbers at the top, indicating number of levels, lives, points, energy, etc. The heads up display is basically game speak for a dashboard that tells you how good you're doing. I assumed that as a manager, you will have seen a dashboard or two in your lifetime, maybe even a score card. These things are not unusual, but in games, they give the individual the power to see how they're doing and where they're doing well, or not as the case may be.

Current technology has enabled organisational leaders to do something similar in the workplace. Typically, the records and statistics we tend to keep are negative, how about instead we all focus on collating and sharing the positives e.g.

praising the percentage of projects that have been achieved, rather than focusing on the negative, and praising attendance rather than focusing on absenteeism. Having access to these statistics shows us where the gaps for improvement are, they become a motivational benchmark.

Dashboards give a person more power and insight into how they can influence what they're doing, how they're being perceived in the organisation, and how well they're doing, even if a manager is not seeing them do a great job because what they do is tracked in the system. Statistics like these also answers the need for instant feedback, both positive and negative. It provides us with a mechanism for people to report if they're in difficulty, or we can see a situation in the dashboard e.g. when progress is not being made in specific areas, we can at a glance identify what help is needed, what input or support is required. Essentially, it becomes more of a trend in general, toward self-management.

Dashboards and clear working objectives combined enable and empower individuals to take charge of their daily work, even their career; it provides them with instant feedback that confirms how well they are doing day in day out. Actually in some gamified performance management systems, people can now place bets at the beginning of the week on things like, which day of the week they're going to have their best possible day. That's based on statistics that are already tracked; how well they're doing against various performance conditions that they've agreed with their manager. It's perceived as a fun thing to do, but sometimes, what we perceive to be our best day, because we woke up happy and feeling 'gung ho' may or may not turn out to be our best day or visa versa, it's just another tool to help our productivity. You could feel horrible, but you end being super productive.

These things happen, but it is fun to actually allow people to see how their progress is affecting the bigger picture, and how their progress in the team is affecting the whole organisation.

I work with a lot of organisations on employee engagement and building these types of strategies. When we're looking at incorporating feedback loops, to help people understand what they're doing well, and where the potential loop holes are, it is amazing what happens. You give them the tools. You communicate the *why* clearly through a proper communication plan. Then you let people self-manage.

Ted Talk presenter, Simon Sinek, in his *On the Power of Why* presentation explains that in order to create loyal followers and active brand ambassadors, you need to give them a compelling reason why, what and how they can buy into something. The same goes for your team and employees the world over. You communicate the *why* clearly enough and then you let people self-manage. You become the support your team needs. Management become the motivators, they spot opportunities for giving genuine and specific feedback, praise and pointers for improvement. Giving praise by catching someone in the moment doing something well offers an employee an amazing piece of reassuring and career affirming communication.

Remember, feedback doesn't have to be a systematic approach, it can be totally random; the key is it has to be genuine, and it has been specific, and ideally, it has to be delivered at the right time to be truly effective.

As long as you give people the value of knowing where they're at and how they're influencing the bigger picture, you'll be making progress together. That's the core of nurturing the power of your people, by understanding what drives them in a positive way towards the best that they can possibly be. It requires you to be an actual real leader, to step up and say "Okay, my vision is we want to achieve X and this is how I will be supporting you, so tell me what else I can do to be a better supporter. Tell me what I need to do to help you"? This is essentially what I did as a manager in the corporate world.

I listened, then I did what we agreed, my role was to lead the vision, then step back until either the agreed time, or I was needed for support. In employee meetings I made sure to check we were OK and when was a reasonable reporting back time for the next stage so I was always in the loop, but they were in charge of their own projects. When they did a great job, I would give them specific praise. If they didn't, I had to step up and be the leader and say something that would get them back on track. When you hire great people, that's exactly what they will do, if you let them.

It's amazing when you give more responsibility away how it alleviates the anxiety of having to know it all, and minimises the fear of being caught out for not knowing enough. If you look after, and really care about your people, and you nurture them throughout their career, it's amazing how you will see them blossom and grow. I challenged you to take up the Gallup 12 question survey to see how you are currently influencing your people. I'm not asking you to look at it just for your company, though it will give you an interesting insight into how things are perceived, but I'm really challenging you to look at it with your manager's hat on and maybe even putting yourself in the shoes of a direct employee by asking yourself "If I was in their shoes, how would I rate me on these 12 questions"?

How would you rate yourself on these 12 questions? Answer through the eyes of a direct employee:

Q. Do I know what is expected of me at work?

A. _____

Q. Do I have the materials and equipment I need to do my work right?

A. _____

Q. At work, do I have the opportunity to do what I do best, every day?

A. _____

Q. In the last seven days, have I received recognition or praise for doing good work?

A. _____

Q. Does my supervisor, or someone at work, seem to care about me as a person?

A. _____

Q. Is there someone at work who encourages my development?

A. _____

Q. At work, do my opinions seem to count?

A. _____

Q. Does the mission/purpose of my company make me feel my job is important?

A. _____

Q. Are my co-workers committed to doing quality work?

A. _____

Q. Do I have a best friend at work?

A. _____

Q. In the last six months, has someone at work talked to me about my progress?

A. _____

Q. This last year, have I had opportunities at work to learn and grow?

A. _____

Give yourself between 1 and 10, one being poor and 10 being absolutely great at communication, then see how you fair and adjust accordingly as your skills develop. To get genuine feedback, who better to ask than your team and your peers, it's called *360-degree feedback*. It's a daring move because you'll be stepping out of your comfort zone by asking them do rate you, but if you can take a few hits to your ego, you'll come out of it the other end a stronger, wiser, more knowledgeable leader, just like they always do on the TV programme *Under Cover Boss*. Remember, it's our ego that makes us control in an autocratic way, so I challenge you to engage with your employees to gain a better understanding of who your people are and what they need from you. Tapping into the real power source starts here with your people.

Tapping into the power of people is an idea whose time has come. People are technology savvy enough to understand self-management related dashboards. Social media are at the core of some of the changes in how we work moving forward; it is influencing how we want to be valued and how we want instant feedback to be part of our lives. People on average want to belong to something that is bigger than themselves, but also where they can be their best possible self. A lot of societies have come to the point in time where the basics are covered as a given; now what we're aiming for is more self-expression, so a more self-actualisation type of approach to life, which includes our working life. It means leadership has to change with it to facilitate what drives the modern worker.

Links:

Gallup images:
- http://home.southernct.edu/~pager1/gallup.htm
- http://www.gallup.com/businessjournal/182321/employees-lot-managers.aspx?g_source=position1&g_medium=related&g_campaign=tiles

Simon Sinek:
- https://www.ted.com/talks/simon_sinek_how_great_leaders_inspire_action

Tapping into the crowd

CHAPTER THREE
STRATEGIC MODELS
SUPPORTING ENGAGEMENT

Tapping into the crowd

For years, strategy models have been focused on process delivery; they also focused on all the key elements positively influencing strategy such as how organisations could put their company on the map. Whether you're in a single location start-up business, or a large multi-nationally based corporation, it is still possible to use many of these strategic models. However, when it comes to setting an organisation up for engagement, these old strategic models leave a lot to be desired.

The most popular models still being taught in MBA and other business courses are *Porter's Five Forces* which has a strong focus for looking externally to the environment, competition and buying power. The *PEST* analysis considers the following external influencing factors: political, economical, social and technological factors. More recently the *Blue Ocean* strategy has entered the mix with a higher focus on innovation as a value creator and differentiator. The great thing about these models is that they all provide solid thinking, so are easily replicated, and they're more process driven and results oriented too.

To name a few of the key strategy models currently in use, some were designed specifically for the industrial era where things tend to be more predictable, and the largest source of income comes from manufacturing, and creating products, as opposed to service based industries where value is created through the provision of valued-based items.

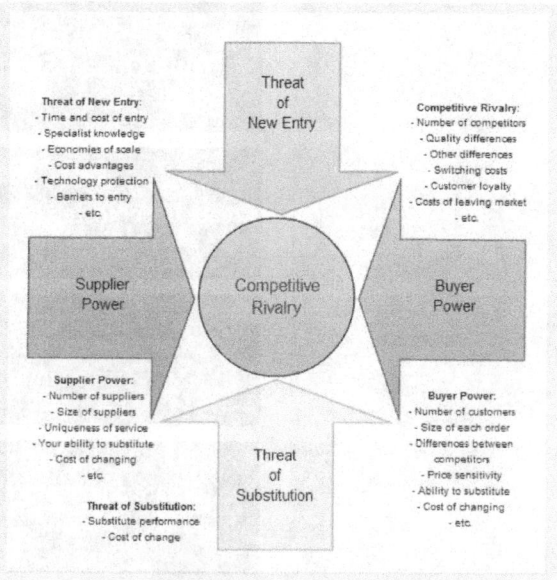

Porter's Five Forces

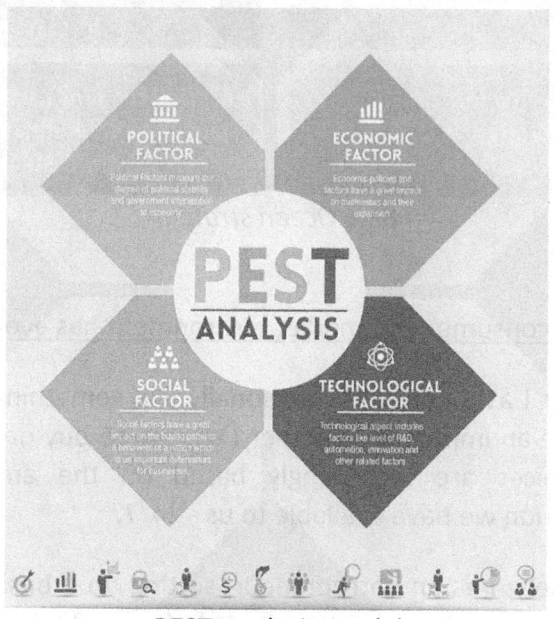

PEST analysis model

Tapping into the crowd

Red Ocean Strategy	Blue Ocean Strategy
Compete in existing market space	Create uncontested market space
Beat the competition	Make the competition irrelevant
Exploit existing demand	Create and capture new demand
Make the value-cost trade-off	Break the value-cost trade-off
Align all the firm's activities with its strategic choice of differentiation or low cost	Align all the firm's activities in pursuit of differentiation and low cost

Blue Ocean strategy

Today's consumer and market environment has evolved.

Whether I as a consumer personally like something or not, will have an impact on whether I choose to buy or not, and our choices are increasingly based on the amount of information we have available to us - 24/7.

Conversely, I as an entrepreneur, setting up a business will also find it easier today than ever before in terms of there

42

being little red tape, or capital needed. Consequently, young people are increasingly choosing this route, rather than working for a large corporation, to achieve their lifestyle goals. Therefore, I think these strategy models, while having proved their worth, now need to be modernised because they lack the human approach. So we need to look at ways of making these models even better by inserting the human dynamic.

When I look, for example, at one of the most popular models I use namely the *SWOT analysis;* the strengths, weaknesses, opportunities, and threats model. I see there is a place for internal and external focused factors; meaning this model can be used by individuals, teams and organisations alike for providing feedback either from their internal customers (employees, peers, colleagues) and external customers (buyers and suppliers).

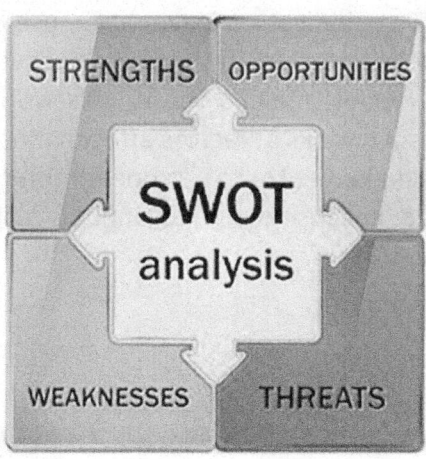

I always look at strengths from all angles so:
✓   the customer's perspective
✓   the employee's perspective
✓   the management team's perspective

✓   the ordinary worker's perspective.

For each corner on strengths, you have 4 different human inputs; the same for opportunities etc.

What your customers see as potential opportunities for your business and your company may be completely different to what your employees see.

However, when you split the employee group opinions from those of management, who no doubt have potentially more access to management data than those on the shop floor who are dealing with your customers, you will again see a completely different point of view. It's the combination of these 4 elements that will actually provide you with a structured view of where human interaction can enhance the strategy models that are currently available.

Key performance indicators have been used to measure operational delivery against strategic objectives and one of the strategic models making these links work is *Balanced Scorecard*. Again it looks at factors affecting the organisation from the outside in, yet there is scope for internal processes to be examined, because their main input is customer driven.

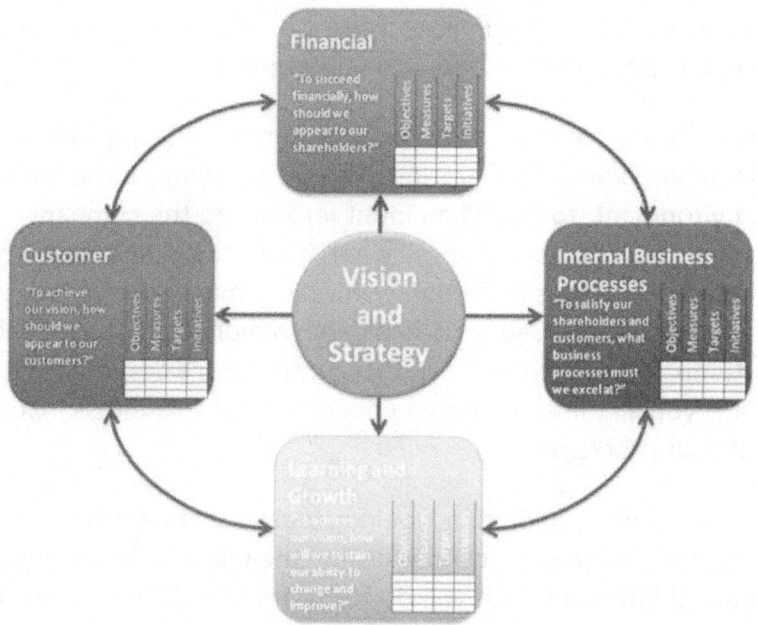

Balanced Scorecard

Models like *Balanced Scorecard* have gone some of the way towards integrating the people factor within organisations. However, it has still received criticism, for not taking into account the specific needs of the people it's aimed at. Even though these systems help, a lot of the time people cannot see the connection of their work to the overall company strategy, or their potential impact on it.

For most people strategy is not something they feel actively involved in unless they are in the C-suite of the company. We often hear the comment *we are only a small cog in a big wheel* meaning they feel they are replaceable. In an age where robots are likely to be able to do a lot more of our work in years to come, combined with the growing uncertainty and increased lack of connection to strategy, or belief that we can influence our organisation's performance is very low. These

45

are not ideal conditions to raise an employee's sense of engagement which is also at an all-time low.

Employees have always craved a sense of being able to influence what they are involved in, from the basic work environment, to having an input into where the company is going, how it does things, what it produces and best to improve client satisfaction. In fact, many client facing employees will see and hear the majority of the initial stumbling block client's experience, so they're best placed to give you all the solutions you need in order to address many of your problems.

Customers, by definition would actually like your product to be the best it can possibly be for their use. They have a vested interest that it will do for them exactly what they it need it to do. But the question is "When your customer gives you feedback, do you listen"? Or do you respond "Oh no, not another one"?

From an employee perspective, they're often the first in line to spot a problem in the customer delivery process, or a problem with the product whether that's due to a management process or something else, such as a product not selling. Likewise, they hear things from the client's perspective about what's working and what's not working. My questions are

Again, if you don't know, I strongly suggest, you need to find out.

In my career to date, I have worked with quite a number of these strategic models in management consulting, thought we usually started with *Balanced Scorecards*. I came from the change management perspective, so would have done a lot of work around creating communication plans, engaging people, and to date, using one of my favourite pieces on change management, which I think needs to be included in every strategy course; *Our Iceberg is Moving*, by John Kotter.

It really shows all the various reactions people have towards change in business. We know by now that change today is inevitable, it's a constant, and technology has sped up change like never before. Technology has made us able to improve and accelerate what we already do well on a daily basis. We have more data available to us in readable formats than ever before. We also have the chance to look up anything we want thanks to the likes of Google and other search engines like Yahoo and Bings.

These sites enable us to have all the information we need at our fingertips, any time we want, in real time. We no longer have to wait around for a business analyst department, or strategic analysis unit to collate and type up the research we want. This means we are able to make informed decision faster than ever, which is what most organisations today have to do. The modern organisation needs to be swift and nimble to stay ahead of the competition.

This becomes more of a challenge when you're a larger corporation? It's a challenge because most of us, and it's borne out by the 80/20 rule, that most human beings go to work to deliver a good day's work, unless they have a grudge about something unresolved be it at home or at work, they not only show up, but they want to give it their best shot on any given day. But when you rely on people, you're dealing with a variable, and from a strategic perspective, that means your employees are key to your competitive advantage, so you need to make them centric to the design of all of your functions, of all of your products, and of all of your services.

Putting employees in the middle of your strategic model puts them in a controlling position, with massive influence over your product and your design, but when you do, you are actually pushing people power back into your business. People power today, combined with crowd sourcing and crowd funding has become a popular way forward.

When you do it right, your business takes off, seemingly, without any particular effort. It's like the wind fills your sail and you're off. You're actually cruising towards whatever goal it is that you have set, assuming you've communicated it to the rest of the crew, your crowd will do the rest as long as what you offer is appealing to them.

Tapping into the crowd is something most strategic models today haven't looked into. Most strategic models only look at your marketplace, external factors, economic factors and political factors. I would argue that the most interesting and most important politics to actually get sorted are the ones coming from within an organisation. I've worked on numerous projects where politics were the stifling factor, not just for creativity and innovation, but also for achieving actual progress. Consequently, employees didn't participate in a meaningful way, and many left. However, without internal political in-fighting, the status quo for the rest of the organisation was actually quite a good place to be.

In an engagement dysfunctional organisational politics are typically rife. I think in some sense you can't but have them. It's one of the human conditions; humans like to belong. Therefore, we seek out people who are similar to us, or have similar views to us because we are always seeking to create allies. We'll obviously also always have opposing parties. Consequently, everything that you do inside an organisation, you will have force field analysis, or force fields taking place; some pulling you away from, some pulling you towards some things. That is critical in human-centred design.

This combined approach to power means employees are corroborating and cooperating, and when they are sufficiently engaged with your vision, it becomes the inevitable secret factor that will set your business apart from your competitors. Things that you may not ever have imagined can become, all of a sudden, true because you have manged to engage people with what matters most to them.

Value-based working has been around for a long time, with the likes of Porter and Kotter having both worked on the theories, such as value chains and value based leadership. Even though many organisations have attempted to implement value based working and leadership, I don't believe anybody in the corporate world has yet truly cracked that nut.

In my experience, when we worked on a project with strengths-based leadership; meaning all management were put through a strengths-based leadership test, as designed by the *Gallup Corporation* in collaboration with Marcus Buckingham, we were looking for value-based strengths. You can take the test in the book *StrengthsFinder 2.0*. The test basically looks at people's strengths which were all value-based. Some people came with strong achievement values, others were creative; others, again optimistic or positive. Every one of us has a combination of the 30 soft values measured in the profile.

Tapping into the crowd

The company that we worked with at the time wanted to implement a strengths-based leadership programme across the board to see if it would drive their teams to succeed as per their vision. The teams that applied it across the board, meaning everyone, found it did work. But those that used it, without following it through, found it ended up being a *nice to have* piece of information, rather than an actual working strategy. Because of the vast difference in implementation success, two years later, the company shelved the programme as too difficult to implement. It took courage to implement a people centric value based working style.

Value-based leadership is often shelved because people don't understand the appeal and don't understand how to implement it. The more analytical models, albeit easier to implement, are still missing the mark for what we need today. As I said earlier, one of the solutions is to develop more feminine leadership traits, if we are to respond to the massive amounts of information, emotions, and change that are coming our way, but then I would bs slightly biased as a business woman to call these feminine traits.

When we look at traditional role models, particularly based in the home, they're mostly women, are that is still true today. However, it is changing in some cultures – gradually. So women have always been used to dealing with multiple factors; otherwise known as juggling. Some days they have a lot of human interaction, others they're managing different budgets and of course, they can't quit, there is no opt out clause, which makes them resilient capable people to have around, which is just as well because like a business, the work never stops.

So we can easily see the similarities between the types of

dynamics needed to run a successful home to those that are required for running a successful business. Whether the leader is a home maker, or a team manager, or even the leader, the multi-tasking over resources to deliver a positive outcome are the same.

Whether it's a corporate or family team, these units work best when they pull together. I love the Kevin Blanchard books, the one that stuck with me is *High 5* where he described a team in a hospital doing a major operation, how the surgeon and the nurses successfully interacted to deliver a specific, smooth process, without ever contemplating what anybody needed to think about. They just did it. Everybody pulled together for the good of the hospital, and of course the patient (their customer), so there were no politics, there is no time or opportunity in a life or death situation.

If we approached business in that same way, then strategic models would actually take more interest into the human condition. With this book, I aim to enable you to play this card more effectively, so you too can pull on the crowd sourcing trend that is so big right now, where people have proven, individually and in groups, that if we can't get financed through the traditional systems, we'll crowd source this instead. Why not use the same tactic for strategy? Strategy and people are the clear link, yet most models still only focus on it as if it were just one element. In my view, it's the one element that impacts all of us; it impacts on our businesses, all our different environments, including political, so impacts on our stability. The impact is so pervasive that we cannot satisfy strategy without including these other human elements also.

When it comes to competition, most of us see competition as

a good thing, a healthy thing. I think in terms of strategy; we're facing more competition than ever before. Even if you're currently operating in a market where you're the trendsetting lone ranger, I guarantee you, if you're doing well; it won't be long before you too have competition.

Competitive advantage is something that most organisations have been searching for, and will continue to search for in years to come. If you have a successful strategy under your hat, that nobody else has, you will be perceived as the disruptive player in the market, and could essentially dominate the marketplace, even for a short time. Competition will always be there.

Even the rules of competition are changing. What used to be acceptable behaviour may now be viewed as aggressive strategies for taking out the other party. Consequently, we see more joint ventures and a move towards a collaborative approach to doing business. I have seen competitors collaborate on a multitude of projects. I personally find entering collaborative agreements with business partners useful and profitable.

Of course there will always be conflicting competitive interests when it comes to sales environments, but isn't it better to spend time serving a client well through a collaboration, rather than spending the time competing. Is it really worth trying to take out your competition? When it comes to human-centred competition, I accept, not everybody likes competition as much as the next person. When we're younger, competing is a game, it is fun; most of us love it. But over time, our appreciation for competition changes, for instance, many managers don't relish the prospect of competing 1-2-1 with their younger staff members for fear of being shown up by these young pups that are coming into the organisation.

Women in particular are not keen to take part in competitions, unless they feel they have a serious chance of competing well. They tend to opt out a lot more than their male counterparts – actually 45% more.

Does that mean women don't engage in competitive behaviour? Of course not, they just display their competitiveness differently. Organisations that are led by women will actually take into account a lot more of the collaborative factors, the softer people factors than their male counterparts have done in the past.

The reality is that most people want the best for themselves, their families and their businesses. However, our history has long since expected men and women to behave somewhat differently. We're both steeped in a default setting that's been trained into us for years and years and it's hard to break some of those ingrained habits and perceptions whether they're true of us or not. For instance, most women have to still do what they need to do when they get home, regardless of what they've just done at work.

The differences in terms of appetite for competition will always vary. Recent statistics have said that age is also a determining factor; that age, in fact, will reduce the uptake and appetite for competition more. I certainly know that having grown older I no longer look at the young competition element the way I used to; in fact, a young competitive streak can be seen as immature even. Today, I look at competition with an element of cynicism and say "They'll learn, the knocks will smooth their rough edges away and they'll learn".

Tapping into the crowd

I don't know if competition is something that we still strive towards, but some people have always had a competitive instinct that is larger than most. Take some political leaders, who want to win more than they want to do their best for those that elected them.

How we perceive competition will also play a part in how we set our competitive strategies. In most organisations, this is not even something that is contemplated. It's maybe not even a topic on the team agenda; no wonder they don't know how to thrive in a competitive market place.

Again, I suggest you go back to your crowd, get some feedback about what you're building, see if they agree they want it, by when, for how much etc. Remember, Ricardo Semler and the Semco Corporation in Brazil, that we discussed earlier, it's what they did to turn their company around. Everything was decided by the employees and the crowd. As a young MBA student at the time, I found their case study a revelation. It was a real eye opener. It made me realise if you give people the power, they will actually convert a failing business into something that is winning because collectively, they can see the bigger picture.

Gamification is the human-centred design of applications, of software, of business processes whereby you use game elements, and game psychology to create positive outcomes. From a strategy point of view, game theory has often been quoted as one of the best ways of getting results, and the military knows that better than most, having used it for years to plan wars and ensure superior strategic positioning.

Increasingly, strategy games are being used to collaborate and build guilds and develop networks in order to achieve a goal. This is not dissimilar to what happens in the corporate sector where teams are playing the game, sometimes against each other, sometimes with each other, but always the name of the game is to create maximum profit for organisations.

Global political and economical uncertainties are changing the dynamics that are driving our core values, both in the corporate world and at home. Individuals are aspiring to achieve personal life goals and dream goal, meaning organisations have to revisit how they are structured to positively engage and retain the right workforce. Start-ups are showing a lot of organisations how this can be done in a rather disruptive way by allowing staff more freedom, more flexibility and more power just by tracking what is essential for the business to achieve.

This tracking is what is also known in the games industry as, the heads up display, as in the game statistics at the top of a game that you're playing, how many lives you have left, how many resources you have left etc. as explained earlier. In a similar way, we see these kinds of techniques coming up in corporate software and corporate processes.

Everybody has heard stories of organisations who allow people the power to set their own schedule, though schemes like flexible working hours, to have their own vacation planning schedule. As long as the work gets done, the rest doesn't really matter. It's a bold step and in order to facilitate it successfully, you do need to put the employee as central to the organisation like Ricardo Semler and Semco did.

It's interesting to see how some organisation daringly go there. The irony of it is that the more freedom people got, the more people want. I believe, in terms of gamification, this is where the key turning points come from in terms of corporate strategy. Why? Because when you do it well, game mechanics will help drive change for the better. It can enable people to give them a sense of freedom, give them a sense of power, and give them a sense of achievement all in one goal.

I think gamification combines motivational theory with game psychology, game dynamics, and game mechanics. It actually grasps a little bit from everything, but at the core, the centre is the human. Just like earlier in the chapter, when we discussed how a *SWOT analysis*, with its 4 levers; one each for the customer, the employee, the manager, and first-line workers all providing their input.

Same with the *Five Forces;* it is in that dynamic process, because no game is static, that the best games are done and the most creatively achieved, all by interacting with others. Same goes for multi-player online games; they're best when there's a group playing together, same deal with board games. People collaborate together in order to achieve the winning goal. People play together for enjoyment and a common goal, all usually produce a winner at the end.

Game theory, on its own is limited, whereas gamification, taking into consideration the wider context like our understanding of neuroscience around what works, how people make decisions, and integrate new values etc. means the games industry has already gotten much right. But there is still room for improvement, and that's the beauty of the games industry, it keeps on trying.

Everything a game encourages you to do is about keeping you focused on moving forward. You fail once, you don't stop playing. You try again, and again, and again, which is what we do in business too, though we don't see as much of that happening. Somewhere down the line there comes a value judgement to say "That was bad", or "You can't do that", or "You're a failure".

When I'm speaking on behalf of European CEO's, I would say "Most of us would view failure as a major negative issue." Even in Asian countries, the Middle East and Europe too, this is not perceived as a positive. I think with the exception of the North Americas where start-up failures are a rite of passage to be qualified for venture capitalism, the rest of the world may not have the same opinion.

To summarise, to create a competitive advantage, the key to success will always be about putting the human element into the middle of any strategy.

In the following chapters we will demonstrate how best to achieve this; why you should even bother, and find the models that are capable of helping you achieving self-empowerment, so you too can achieve collaboration, and become an evolving leader of the future.

Recommended reading:
➤   High Five – Blanchard
➤   Our iceberg is melting –John Kotter
➤   StrengthsFinder 2.0 – Marcus Buckingham
➤   Maverick – Ricardo Semler

Tapping into the crowd

CHAPTER FOUR
KNOW YOUR CROWD

Tapping into the crowd

When we decide to tap into a particular crowd, it's important we know what and who we are tapping into, and why they have become our target market. So let's explore who the current and future workforce consists of, then we'll aim to get a better understanding of what drives them, especially their likes, dislikes, and how to communicate with them.

The workforce consists of a mix of people:
- mature baby boomers (1945-1960)
- Generation X (1961-1980)
- Generation Y (1981–1995), sometimes called millennials, and last but not least,
- Generation Z (born after 1995).

Most generations are defined by the events that shaped their era, be they social, economic, political or environmental. For example, the baby boomers saw in the introduction of television as one of the biggest domestic inventions of their day. Their parents were the first to drives cars and have telephones installed at home. Typically, they grew up in more organisational, industrialised and hierarchical structures. Respect for their elders and authority in general would have helped them make sense of the amazing changes they were living through.

From a communication perspective, whilst they are not averse to being online, the tendency is for have face-to-face interaction, and when work requires them to go online, be prepared to have the webcam on so they can see you. While some of this generation still has energy left to continue working, many more are thinking of retirement, meaning, the vast majority of todays' workers are made up of Generation X and Y.

Generation X experienced historic events such as the fall of the Berlin Wall, Thatcherism, and the Cold War ending. Politically, they lived through offices held by Reagan, Gorbachev, and the Clintons to name but a few.

It was this period that saw the birth of *Pong*, the first computer game, released in the early '70s. There have been subsequent evolutions in development of computers and game consoles ever since. In fact, the introduction of mobile technology and the personal computer is probably the biggest invention of their time. They saw Bill Gates come out with *Microsoft* and Steve Jobs with *Apple*, so they'll be aware of these two inspirational entrepreneurs significant to their era.

This generation love technology. They can't imagine not having emails and text messaging, so it's no surprise to discover they have a preference for communicating this way, rather than the more traditional face-to-face approach preferred by the baby boomers. However, this group will happily slip in and out of both modes of communication quite naturally.

Generation Y, mostly experienced economic boom times, but they've also seen real terror with events such as 9/11, the Taliban, and the rise of ISIS. Social media came into existence when they were growing up, so they are used to sharing, everything, even inappropriate material (that older generations would probably have shared privately), all without realising the consequences of their actions; it is hard to make material disappear once it has been posted on the world wide net.

Game consoles and controllers became smaller and we saw

many evolutions from x-Boxes, PS1 to PS3, from Nintendo DS to Nintendo WII's and smartphone and tablet based games. Game genres continued to expand from multi-player online games, to role playing games, first person shooters, adventures etc. Casual gaming became a widespread phenomenon with games like *Angry Bird* and *Candy Crush* to name the two biggest success stories.

Reality TV became all the rage, Smart phones and other mobile devices such as tablets became intimate communication tools these people couldn't imagine being without. Their natural default setting is to type a text, or tweet on social media, rather than have a phone or face-to-face conversation. Of course in a business context, face-to-face interaction is still an essential requirement for most decision making situations, even if the lead up is primarily conducted online.

Whilst Generation Y, mostly grew up during boom times, Generation Z wasn't so fortunate. They came into the world during a global economic downturn. They have seen what happens to banks and large corporations during an economic downturn, they have heard of *WikiLeaks*, although it blew up when they were still young, and they have experienced first-hand how the *lack* of funds influences all other areas of their life.

They probably learned to swipe a mobile device before they learned to read, growing up as they do, with a tablet and Smart phone in their hand. They live on mobile devices and cloud computing. So devices they aspire to owning include wearables like *Fitbits*, *3D headsets* like *Google Cardboard* and *Oculus Rift and Gear VR, Samsung VR,* augmented reality headsets such as *HoloLens*, 3D printing and whatever other must have new gadgets are coming out. It is very likely that they have tried out Pokemon Go, which brought augmented reality and gamified walking to a mass market thanks to an ingenious combination of two existing games namely Ingress and Pokemon and two technologies namely augmented reality and geolocation.

Their communication devices are mobile, WIFI connected and they think nothing of communicating via text, social chat rooms with emoji's, or tweeting in 140 characters or less on sites such as *Snapchat* and *Instagram* rather than just *Twitter or Facebook*. Their solutions of preference are digital and crowdsourced. They aim to run their own business instead of joining an established company. This is an interesting development, but not exactly a surprise considering the perception of non-existent job-security today. From a corporate perspective, it means you as a manager have to work even harder to engage with these entrepreneurial types, and you will need to adopt a different approach to keeping them on board too.

Generation Y spends money boldly with few boundaries because they grew up within an economic boom when pocket money was freely given because both parents worked. Conversely, Generation Z is showing greater financial restraint and economic awareness with 57% of them saving money, probably the result of an experience with family members not having a regular income.

Generation Y are consumers, they spend their leisure time shopping, hanging out with friends in shopping centres, and going to cinemas or bowling. Generation Z on the other hand, are more selective in their choices and prefers to shop virtually, so make most of their shopping purchases online.

Tapping into the crowd

Age, stage of development and personal situations have always shaped how each generation views their world, never more so than Generation Y and Generation Z who are living in an increasingly volatile and complex society structure, compounded by recession, terrorism, and violence.

Generation Y subscribe to everything social, unlike Generation Z who prefers sites such as *Snapchat, Secrets* or *Whispers* to communicate. They tend to be selective over the type of content they share and who they share it with, while Generation Y enjoys a *free for all,* not minding who is tracking what, not least because their parents are mostly late joiners to social channels, so most of what they did went un-supervised such as parties with friends, holiday relationships to other documented social exploits. Generation Z on the other hand is a lot more secretive, and would rather not be tracked or traceable.

Generation Y watches *YouTube, Hulu, Netflix*, etc. Generation Z wants to co-create Livestream and make up the content as they go. Recently, game franchise *Mario Bros* came out with its *Super Mario Maker*, whilst the original series of *Super Mario* games are out significantly longer. *Super Mario Maker* allows players to create their own *Super Mario* game. Another game favoured by this generation is *Minecraft,* which is an infinite open ended game where you create a world with blocks online (a bit like *Lego* but online - not a physical brick in sight). A lot of children have taken to *Minecraft* to create things such as their own books and instruction guides, which enables their friends to play better too. This group has an expectation and mentality that lends itself to co-creation, be it in education, the home, or the workplace.

Generation Y loves sports and taking part in extreme adventures. Generation Z sees sports as a healthy tool that you need to do, but it is not play. Their games are based indoors in terms of computers, tablets, online devices and the VR and AR as reality tools used for some of their favourite games.

One of the consequences of this lifestyle is the growing problem of teen obesity. In fact, it has tripled since the 1970s, particularly amongst Generation Z, though Generation Y isn't immune; both are suffering with inferior health due to poor lifestyle choices. Health experts even predict this will be the first generation to be buried by their parents instead of the other way around.

While the recent craze of *Pokemon Go* (a combination of gaming and walking) has rekindled a childhood game for many Generation Y and introduces a new game to generation Z players; it provides a real option and opportunity to make gamified exercise more widespread. Since the success of Pokemon Go, Mario Bros is currently working on Mario Run, a platform game that enables you to jump over obstacles and hurdles to get better.

Generation Y grew up with a slightly longer attention span- about the average length of a TV commercial. Generation Z's attention span is reported to be even shorter with some researchers having recently quoted it as around eight seconds. Personally I would say that this is probably a bit short; this generation are by definition, based on their passion, already masters of multitasking. They have grown-up with multiple feeds and streams of information on multiple devices all vying for their attention. Accordingly, this generation is used to juggling, but it has probably resulted in them being perceived as hyperactive in terms of relating to people and their surroundings.

Generation Y love text messages as the norm, while Generation Z, loves to communicate through images, icons and symbols. It's interesting to observe how this is evolving and what the future of the workforce will do to accommodate this new breed of employee. It is already shaping how we communicate in business and how much more we are prepared to instigate change through images and icons. For example, *Hashtags (#)* are a popular way of organising information; having a *hashtag* makes your topic searchable, and easier to find by like-minded online tribes.

Generation Y worried about growing their social status and gaining *likes,* retweets and followers, while Generation Z worries more about how the economy is influencing their environment, apparently, the need to control ones' destiny is stronger for the younger generation.

Generation Y enjoyed a life that basically revolved around them. Many of them had both parents working full-time. Whether out of guilt from not being there, or simply having the financial means, meant this was a generation that grew up with parents who could afford to give their children everything they wanted to. Their child was very much central to everything. To nobody's surprise this created a generation with *Planet Me* as their focus with a strong need to always know *what's in it for me* before taking action.

By contrast, Generation Z has had to get used to coping in fragmented households, where several generations live together for economic reasons. Siblings often have different parents, or surrogate or adoptive parents because biological parents didn't get married, or have divorced and remarried. They are used to adapting and dealing with different numbers of people looking after them, which probably accounts for them being a more self-reliant generation. *Sparks & Honey* research found that Generation Z cope better with reality compared to Generation Y who are pre-occupied with escaping reality by creating a virtual reality.

Behavioural marketing analysts have for a long time realised the influence of younger generations from buying decisions relating to dinner menus, vacations, home furnishings and even family cars. Three out of four in this generation would prefer to make their current hobby their full-time job. That's a lot more than the Generation Y would have said. If Generation Y are choosy about what job they take, Generation Z will be even more so.

Generation Z is not necessarily interested in generating social celebrity status or repining and retweeting things. Generation Z is all about creating new things, so they edit photos and videos putting their own unique stamp on them. They may just have one picture in *Snapchat,* which they send to one friend, while Generation Y tend to post all their pictures on all their social media channels from *Facebook* to *Twitter* to *Instagram,* etc. to show them off to as many of their followers as possible.

Generation Z are all about creating new information that is useful to them in their spare time such as video production and app development. They are also by definition entrepreneurial, with 61% of this group considering entrepreneurialism as a career option, rather than taking a job in the corporate sector. This is a key statistic for employers to consider, because it means they can't force this generation to fit into a rigid structure as it could result in them leaving, feeling disengaged and robbed of their freedom and creativity. "I don't want your traditional ways of working, I'll create my own, thank you very much", is a statement you could expect to hear from an unfulfilled Generation Z worker.

Generation Z grew up with high definition video and photographs, they like touchscreen, *iPhones* with icons, so they favour visual sites and they think in pictures and emoji's, videos and GIF's. They will make up conversations with images rather than long amounts of text. In content production terms this is what we call *snack able*. It's an analogy for eating a snack in a few minutes; hence *snack able* content because it is also consumed in a few minutes; short and sweet, just like the audience's attention span.

Generation Z tends to engage in social listening, tapping into news and information channels; they know about key issues that are affecting our planet, they know about gender inequality, the rising cost of education, environmental issues and so forth. Consequently, they tend to be activists, more so than previous generations. Up to 80% believe we need to do something drastic about issues such as global warming, and 26% of them want to go into volunteering, which is higher than in previous generations. That doesn't mean they may not set up a social enterprise at some point, it just means that when they do, it is more likely to be congruent with their entrepreneurial spirit.

Their learning style is forcing change on traditional education. They consciously choose not to stick with the traditional methods of learning in favour of quick byte sized information. They learn by doing and creating with trial and error as their feedback system. Listening to endless lectures with professors reeling off their wisdom, followed at some point by a written exam is too old school for them.

Generation Y was prone to being influenced by reality TV, celebrities and pop-stars, with Generation X before them even more so. However, Generation Z looks for input and influence from their immediate circle of friends, rather than celebrities per se. They prefer personalised experiences as validated by their friends. Peer-to-peer recommendation is more important than celebrity endorsement. *YouTube* stars they can relate to and peer reviews are what influences Generation Z, especially when presented in a fun and engaging way. Yes they are attached to their mobile devices, but they still want to connect with real people; they want to see real people in advertisements as opposed to celebrities. For example, YouTubers like *PewDiePie* (with around 40 million subscribers) have created a major following because they are real and funny, and they often started out as average Joes' so they are easy to relate to. Conventions where they can connect with these people in person are important, so Generation Z spends more than three hours a day on their computers for non-school, non-work related activities.

All the same, they are a contradictive bunch because whilst we know that video shapes their opinions, they also enjoy meeting their favourite stars and sharing these photos and other selfies with selected friends. This is just part of growing up, the majority of us did it, the difference is that today, thanks to social media, it's much easier to share and reach a wider audience if you choose to.

When I speak to managers in the baby boomer and Generation X age groups, they tell me one of their biggest challenges is understanding how to engage with Generation Y and Z. Generation Z are self-starters and creators, so want their creativity and individuality recognised, whereas Generation Y wants to know *what's in it for me.* So one group are motivated by their progress, recognition and achievement, the other wants to make a difference and improve the world. These differences will continue to be reflected in their job choices and the start-ups these generations make.

Generation Y wants to know how to take the next step in their career and fulfil their potential. Generation Z wants to see how their role is making a difference to the company and the wider world. Understanding these differences will become critical to a successful manager. For example, when answering questions arising during job interviews that reflect these generational differences. So, being flexible about how you communicate and deal with people from both these generations will rely on noticing the small things that make a big difference. I believe managers need to adopt an open-mind and willingness to adapt their style, one that also responds to being challenged.

By understanding these subtle differences, businesses will become better informed about how to deliver their message in a way that speaks to their target audience, how these messages are being received, and what to do to attract the best employees, as well as gain their buy-in to keep them engaged so they get a return on their investment.

Be flexible and get ready to change, or expect to have change force upon you is probably good advice, because the workplace and workforce is definitely changing. Therefore, the nature of how we structure our communication, and how we do business will also change. Trying to apply old rules to new situations will not work. So be prepared to disrupt your ways, or you will be disrupted by young upstarts - just as previous generation have always done.

There will always be exceptions to the rule, so this is only a reflection of changing trends, rather than a definitive guide into exact behaviours.

Reference links:

- http://sproutsocial.com/insights/gen-z-vs-gen-y/
- http://www.slideshare.net/sparksandhoney/generation-z-final-june-17
- http://www.huffingtonpost.com/tim-elmore/contrasting-generation-y-_b_5679434.html

Tapping into the crowd

CHAPTER FIVE
THE CHANGING NATURE
OF THE ORGANISATION

Tapping into the crowd

We discussed in the previous chapter how the nature of the workforce is changing, which means the nature of organisational design is also changing, because when people change, by definition, structures change too. Also, the way we access information is driving change. We are seeing a change towards more receptive, more adaptive, and more generative organisational structures where the continuous focus is on meeting the needs of all stakeholders: customers, employees, the board, the shareholders, et cetera.

This trend is an evolution towards stronger employee involvement, with people at the top, listening to what's actually happening at the coalface – the base level in organisations. Instead of traditional management hierarchies, organisations are becoming increasingly flatter in nature. Meaning, the power to decide has become much more self-organised and autonomous than it ever was previously. For example, remote workers and virtual teams tend to be self-managing.

Organisations are also increasingly organic in nature; there are less rules and regulations. Some have no real clear boundaries, so they experience constant changing forms and shapes. While this type of evolution sounds counterintuitive to some traditional businesses, it is nevertheless, what the workforce of today is looking for. It is what we're already seeing in successful companies as voted in the 'Best Employer' awards.

Every year for the last five years, *Google* has been ranked at the top of the best places to work, or should that read *Alphabet,* for many good reasons:

I.   They have consistently demonstrated an adaptive approach, which enables self-organised teams to contribute.

II.   They have an evolving organisational structure.

III.   They provide human centric policies across the whole organisation.

IV.   Decisions are often made by the people who know best because they are in a particular role and are considered the most knowledgeable, because they work in the area daily. Consequently, these people are best placed to recognise what is important, as opposed to a management dictating what and how things will be done.

For more traditional business models this represents quite a shift in direction, while others have already taken steps to head in this new direction. A direction where the functionality of authority is increasingly based on capability and experience, rather than titles, status, or years of tenure. It's now about being the right person to make a decision because of having the most relevant knowledge about the topic.

The nature of new organisations relies a lot more on alliances, basic things like collaborating and networking. Even strategic alliances with partners that help you deliver a service, remember the Uber example where they have car owners as a strategic alliance in order for Uber to deliver the taxi service to their clients. Additionally, the tracking capabilities of a collaboration is measured more effectively because it is based on agreed work standards, as opposed to being managed by titles who aren't at the coalface.

These days, teams can exist with a virtual rather than a physical set-up, meaning a lot of people work together, yet remain multi-locational. Some people will be working from home, others will be working in different parts of the world. The nature of the working day is no longer the standard 9 to 5, instead it depends on how your team is constructed. Teams tend to share activities to take advantage of this, so work around what works best for the majority of the team and keeps the team on track. The key to the success of this arrangement, is that everybody, at any given time knows what they are doing, who is responsible for what and by when, including how their role impacts the rest of the project, meaning expectations have to be clearly defined.

Organisations of the future will be flatter, decentralised, and with less middle management. The result is top management will be exchanging more feedback with more people, so systems have to be put in place, and proven to work to allow people to communicate more effectively. It also means that a manager is no longer expected to give input to every single project, but rather expects the people in charge of a delivering a particular project, product or service, will do what needs to be done to get the job done. The statistics based on logged evidence of activity will be what drives decisions.

One of our business partners *MyObjectives* offers a tracking tool based on a combination of the Balanced Scorecard Methodology and Objectives and Key Results (OKR), which is practiced by large corporations to stimulate performance and productivity. Effectively, each employee can see how they are doing against their agreed objectives on screen. Achievement in the success zone results in fun encouragement and feedback. Because managers at all levels also have a view of the same information in real time, their role of reinforcing great activity towards company objectives is made that much easier.

In a modern, future focused organisation it will also mean that individuals are free to roam about the organisation and pitch their skills to new teams or seek new roles to be part of projects and teams that match their skill set. It does require a certain amount of self-initiative to promote yourself, your skills et cetera, and to be able to take on board, or be taken on board by a new team rather than staying static. It also requires good communication skills to share information and give feedback - these are the skills organisations of the future are looking for and value. This level of communication encourages teams to morph together and deliver even more products and services, thus potentially creating a more sustainable competitive advantage.

Success also require an element of mindfulness. Mindfulness asks all team members to be aware of the impact they're having on one another – to always consider the big picture. Equally, to understand the consequences of not delivering what was promised, so a strong understanding of what the knock-on effect is on others in an organisation is important.

The systems we have access to today, combined with the data we are able to extract today, from activities such as market feedback, sales, production all enable us see what patterns are trending. This trend will also be referred to as *Big Data*. Data analysis makes sense of future opportunities as well as learning from feedback.

Data feedback implicitly requires an organisation to become a learning organisation, because by definition, we're learning new things by encouraging information sharing, as well as analysing feedback from our environment. Combined with being more self-organising, internal processes are the support structure built around feedback from the environment. When we look at how nature works in response to whatever challenge arises, it always finds another way. For example, a tree comes into contact with a road, either the root uproots through the road, or it burrows deep underneath the road. The tree will always find a way to continue its growth, humans putting a road in its way isn't going to stunt its progress. As one of my early mentors said "Strategy needs to think like water. Water always finds a way through. Sometimes it's over, sometimes it's around, and sometimes it's through erosion over time, but nothing will stop water finding its own way".

Strategy is the same. It's one of those topics that will go everywhere, and it will drive change over time, even if it sometimes becomes stuck in a repetitive pattern, or temporarily loses impact. In order to remain focused, we need to create some tension between ease of achievement, and the challenge to grow, both of which allows an individual to go over, under, around, or through and flow again. When you swap your traditional strategy from being hierarchically structured, to one that is more people and data powered, you'll need to be a strong leader, or become a strong leader to successfully pull this switch off, when you do, then things will flow like water.

Earlier, we explored the merits of the people centred approach as adopted by the Brazilian organisation Semco. Subsequently, Zappos has taken this approach to a new level. Since 2013, they have been actively implementing the whole practice of holacracy. For example, in the area of job descriptions, in a holacracy there are none, just roles, which are defined around work and responsibilities, and they're updated regularly, as opposed to traditional job descriptions that tend to be precise, are rarely updated, and in a lot of cases irrelevant or outdated.

In a traditional company we may see multiple layers of management; they are all delegating work, and they all retain their right to veto decisions. In a holacracy that authority is totally distributed to the teams and individuals actually doing the work. Decisions are made locally by the people that actually deliver the various tasks required to reach a successful outcome. With big data feedback built into a strategy, the need to micro-manage will disappear, and the need to motivate and cheer on success will only increase. Even Ricardo Semler often found it hard not to interfere, so whilst this strategy is a great objective to aim for, it is also not the easiest to follow through, or put into daily practise.

In traditional companies when embarking on a change of this nature, the organisational structure is rarely revisited and it remains mandated from the top. Many of the change management programmes I used to be involved in were very much driven by the top down, and that's still a true state of affairs for many multinational organisations today. In a holacracy you'll find rapid iterations, an organisational structure that is actually rather fluid, and regularly updated, and every team will have a version of their self-organised team all working together.

A holacracy is the total flipside of traditional companies where you'll find office politics and too many chiefs deciding and influencing internal networks that emerge from *old boys' clubs* to *mean girls* very powerful people in the background running the show. We know that knowledge equals power and people *in the know* or who have access to a power source can actually play games with the rest of the workforce. This kind of set-up is toxic, yet rife, as you will see when you scratch below the glossy PR surface. Websites like *Glassdoor* are feared by managers and HR professionals, because it gives ex-employees a platform to air their views on your company. The site is seen as a feedback tool for measuring organisations with bad practices as a standard. Great companies will still receive great reviews. The website has also become a valuable resource for job seekers to find information about potential employers.

In a holacracy the transparency is what drives everything. Everyone is bound by the same rules regardless or tenure, regardless of position, including CEOs, and the rules are visible to all. If I wanted to check what my CEO was up to, I could see how accountable he was in his roles and responsibilities. For a lot of companies, a holacracy based strategy could be a step too far. Even Zappos HR department said something along the lines of; after 18 months they were still not completely ready to call themselves a holacracy, because they were still evolving. This is a long term strategy, not something you achieve overnight.

Change or transformation of this nature will take time and nurturing. Any approach I've taken with gamification design where we tapped into the crowd and we crowd resourced, took time to:
a)   gain trust and
b)   gain buy-in and
c)   change behaviour.

Because it's about creating behavioural change on multiple levels, from the managerial perspective, down to the perspective of each employee.

If you've been traditionally brought up to work under

command and control type rules - in fact most schools are training us to accept commands from a teacher in readiness to later accept them from a boss - having to all of a sudden decide for yourself and to act to the best of your ability can be quite scary. This transition into a place of uncertainty often provokes a feeling of wanting to go back to the safety of being guided and saying "Well, if I don't need to make the decision, I won't take the hit for it". To transition successfully, we need to accept some people will step up to the challenge, while others will not feel up to this kind of decision making and may leave.

In fact, the transition for Zappos to becoming more holacractic meant about 15% of their people left. That means 85% of their people not only stayed and went with the flow, but stayed for the long run. Zappos implemented a two question approach to management decision making:
1.   Is it safe enough to try? If yes, the second question was
2.   Is there any reason why it could cause us harm e.g. take us backwards, or harm someone's role, do harm to the company, do harm to the service?

The data that was carrying the most authority, was the data from the circle where this proposal actually came from. Any change proposed can come from anywhere within the organisation, but those working closest to it, held the greatest weight in the decision making process. However, if you could provide good data why something would potentially cause harm, then new decisions could be considered.

Compare this to a more traditional structure where everybody has to reach consensus. Giving more weight to the coalface because they are in the know could speed up decision making and speed up the implementation too. This is in contrast to multiple rounds of voting, multiple rounds of consensus seeking and buying-in support, all of which takes up valuable time.

Giving decision making ability to the employees carrying out work comes with accountability for the jobs that need to be completed and roles that need to be performed. In this context, what is being tracked is the accountability and delivery of projects, roles and jobs.

With current information systems, and I'm thinking specifically at some of the evolving performance management systems that are out there, including game mechanics and game dynamics, we are seeing a shift towards full transparency, and full accountability across the board. Also full accessibility of different points of view, so if I need input from another team in order to make an educated decision, the infrastructure is now there to help me do that.

Flatter structures obviously have less middle management to a totally flat organisation where there is no manager per se, they have a web like structure, where different networks actually work together to deliver the greater goal. These flatarchies are a combination of a hierarchy and a flat structure where you still have teams reporting in to the management. It's by combining that networking structure, with a flat organisation and, a hierarchical organisation that creates the hybrid of all 3 detailed above, as illustrated in the image below.

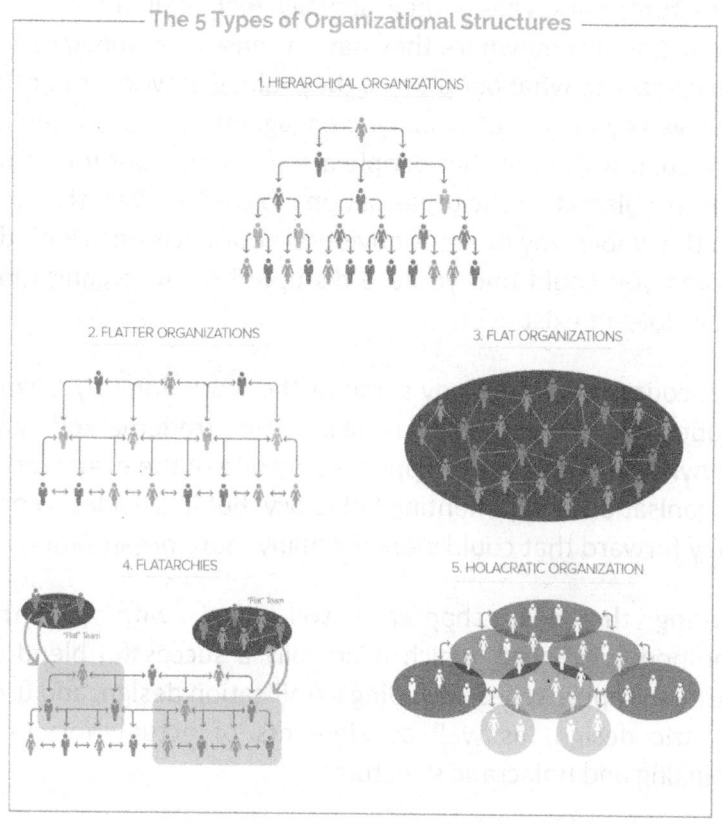

© Jacob Morgan (thefutureorganization.com)

I think it's an interesting concept. It's where a lot of organisations will end up and will probably be most comfortable. Then there will be an emergence of more holacratic organisations working in circles towards specific goals with very clear purposes. I would challenge you to examine what's possible within your organisation and within your team.

We have to accept that the nature of the current workforce is asking you for a more holacratic, more flat organisational structure; somewhere they actually feel their influence is valued, and somewhere they have a sense of belonging. So, going back to what people said they valued at work as per the twelve key factors of employee engagement, as reported by Gallup, it is evident that people are screaming out for more, flatter holacratic style organisations to work in. Whether you go the whole way or not is obviously your decision. Don't do it and you could find you are disrupted by an organisation that doesn't exist - yet.

I encourage you to study some of the work done by Brian J Robertson around holacracies. He trademarked and copyrighted the term. Zappos is only one of the examples of organisations implementing holacracy, but it is evidently one way forward that could work for many more organisations.

During the next chapter I will share with you the methodology I use, which is actually a successful blend of strategic approaches, including gamification design, and user centric design, as well as elements of actual holacratic thinking and holacratic structures.

CHAPTER SIX
CROWDSOURCING
EMPLOYEE ENGAGEMENT

Tapping into the crowd

Introducing gamification starts with strategy, and in my view, gamification, or applying game psychology, game elements and game mechanics, in non-game situations has always been played in business.

Where possible, I start gamification conversations at C-level, because often VP's hold decision making power over their teams. Tapping into this level is especially important when embarking on a companywide transformation strategy; change has to be driven from the top down. Management needs to be actively seen to engage and support behaviour change for it to permeate the whole organisation.

Implementation of a gamification programme typically starts in one of two ways:
1. either through the company in one go, or
2. as a pilot test within a team that is representational of the company.

As a decision maker, your courage and knowledge of the business is what will determine the best approach. It takes input and buy-in from the whole organisation over a period of time to make it work for everyone. Remember Zappos in the previous chapter, they started with one team, before gradually letting it infiltrate the whole company. Even if you are not the CEO, as long as you are a VP or senior manager, you can still implement it within your team. When other department heads start hearing and seeing the successes coming from your area, I know you will receive inquiries as to how they can replicate it in their teams too.

A Norwegian organisation I worked with wanted to use a change management process to up-date and embed its new vision. They were losing market share, and at number three in the market, they were dropping significantly in popularity.

The CEO wanted their vision to change from being a traditionally focused organisation, to a more forward thinking one, by tapping into national cultures and national values. The timing was during the aftermath of the incident with mass shooter Breivik, so the person on the street was pre-occupied with what was happening to Norwegian values and Norwegian pride. It was tapping into the value of being *one with nature*, to being the happy, friendly type of personalities that they typically are. Having spent a lot of time there, I can vouch for that. The CEO wanted his company to offer a fresh dynamic and young take on this theme.

Everything the company delivered in terms of services had to fall into that new vision; how they worked together, and how they treated customers. The management team had carried out market research of what was living, and what was being said about the company, and decided on how their vision needed changing going forwards. The CEO of the team approached me and said "Look, we need change. We need to drive change from the inside to the rest of the teams, but I want everyone to be on board. I don't want there to be any confusion. I want the message to be very clear, but I'm not hung up on the how. I want to create something we can all be proud of.

Having a clear *why* is actually mission critical to applying any new approach. What did we do with my Norwegian client? We always start with asking *why* questions, so my approach is to always ask the management team "Why are we embarking on this road? Why are we changing the way we're working to this new way of working"? You need to have established your vision to be able to answer these questions.

Then we presented the new vision, explaining the reasons

why this was important to each team. Companies that understand the *why* tend to have a stronger connection with their employees and customers; some even create a loyal fan base.

Part of that first step is about understanding *why* we are even changing direction and *why* that change is important to the whole company? So we invited each team to provide input on how they would deliver this new vision and to explain what it looks like. They answered questions like: how will we deliver our service? What will it mean for my customers? How will it influence internal customer relations and processes amongst colleagues?

Each team had time to reflect and think "Okay, this is how we think we should be doing". Then, each team was invited in a companywide SWOT 360. A SWOT 360 is basically the strengths, weaknesses, opportunities and threats analysis, as applied to their team. The first step is a team self-reflection exercise to gain an understanding of how we as a team view ourselves, and what our strengths and weaknesses are, including opportunities and threats we know exist.

Each team works together and comes up with their own SWOT 360 analysis. This is a big paper exercise, flip charts, the works, lots of colours, lots of noise, lots of debate. The whole company in different team huddles around the room. The atmosphere was a buzz because everybody was seen working on one vision. That in its own right created an interesting dynamic that you often experience in multi-player online games where you're actually working towards a common goal.

We purposely asked managers to be part of the management

team, rather than their respective operational teams, only returning to their business unit after they had completed their SWOT 360 analysis. Seeing teams self-organise has to be seen to be believed. This is why playing games is so empowering, seeing your colleagues fighting in your corner creates an amazing experience for all. Even when real, visible, tangible fears arose; it was still something that was dealt with positively. It was fun to watch.

When each team had completed their SWOT 360, we asked them to swap their flipchart with another team who reviewed the results, and added even more feedback. The only rule was to only write what you're willing to stand up and say to someone's face. That was a good enough rule to curb any political division and limit random attacks of negativity. By focusing only on constructive feedback, which is essential in this kind of exercise, it helps people to be the best version of themselves. Anyone unwilling to clarify their feedback publicly had it scrapped.

The whole focus was based on the greater good of the company, rather than the individual parts. This minimises personal battles or whims being aired. The key focus is around what needs to happen to change and manage new processes. Setting people up for success in this exercise is absolutely essential, as is setting them up to know it is OK to be honest. We had the CEO stand up and give his permission by saying "I want your feedback and I want you to be honest." In Nordic countries, getting people to be honest doesn't tent to be a big deal, they are by nature that way inclined, so will usually tell it like it is.

Obviously, this is not the same in every culture. For example, in the UK, asking for honesty will often prompt an apology, followed by a watered down version of the truth as the British are fairly reticent about being honest for fear of hurting someone's feelings. Where there are cultural differences like these, I would encourage clarification by creatively asking for specifics. We can even if required, set these processes up on a system's based scenario, but the rules remain the same; if someone isn't willing to say something face to face, they don't write their feedback down or the feedback is eliminated.

The swapping of the SWOT 360 provides other departments input on each and every element of the company, including the management team. Because I had kept the management team together, allowing teams to self-organise, I often saw managers looking and straining to hear if their teams were doing the right thing. They needn't have worried, most teams, especially those with lots of skills, and years of experience were actually quite keen to deliver good work and put their best ideas forward.

At the end of the process, everyone's flip charts were displayed on the wall. Everyone walked around reading them, but without discussion. Feedback is only feedback; some you own and you can change, and some is outside your power to control. We moved through each team, starting with the management team, and asked them to reflect on the feedback that they had received, as well as be thankful and grateful for people being honest about how they perceived them. Also, to appreciate the feedback, even if the feedback wasn't positive, jut be thankful, and open minded about receiving it.

No defending was allowed either, there was no place at that particular point for defending why anyone did something a certain way, or why something happens a certain way. That would be the default in any given situation whereby, if there was any negative criticism, people could go into a defensive mode, especially the management team.

We asked for clarification on the points that they didn't understand, or how perceptions were maybe different in other departments about their team, and what did that mean. Clarification was allowed, and then thankfulness.

On completion of this intense exercise, which took a day, teams retained their own flip charts to help them develop and evaluate their plans. The company as a whole had agreed a new set of action plans, business aims and objectives to implement.

We ended with a big celebration for all that we'd achieved.

This exercise is an extremely powerful opportunity to make sure everyone is aligned to the company's goals and vision. It requires an experienced facilitator for a successful outcome, often they act as a translator for potentially contentious issues and a reminder of the rules of the game to keep the SWOT 360 big picture focused and the feedback session simply clarification focused.

After the SWOT 360 day, it is important to maintain momentum by drilling down actions into specific KPI's and business objectives, assigning different roles to different teams, getting specific jobs approved. It also provided them with a clear framework as to what do we take on and what don't we take on? What specific projects are good for us and are aligned with this new strategy, what is not? What approaches that we are currently using in sales and marketing are no longer fitting?

This internal crowdsourcing process is what I call 'hard fun'. Hard because feedback often points out serious or difficult issues that need addressing, and fun because of the atmosphere that can be created when teams pull together. When the CEO and facilitator set the tone, and the management team is seen to be having fun, then most of the other teams will want to join in too.

Reinforcing a transformation will need you to create new heroes, new rituals and new stories to make your new culture stick. So look for internal success stories, potential heroes and legacies. You may find inspiration from other successful cultures to help you though your transition period, but ultimately new stories come from within. Corporate culture is built through rituals, and stories of amazing characters that have worked for us. For example, the culture of *Virgin* wouldn't be the same if it wasn't for Richard Branson. He doesn't work every day in the business anymore, but how the company is structured is because of this hero character that shaped the adventurous spirit and customer focus led company he is best known for. Consequently, his successful approach and methodologies have been well documented and mirrored.

Reference:
For more information on that all important why question, I highly recommend a TED Talk by Simon Sinek, called *'The Power of Why'*.

CHAPTER SEVEN
GAMIFICATION
DESIGN THINKING

Tapping into the crowd

To build on the crowdsourcing workshop, I assist attendees to clarify their gamification design strategy to accompany the SWOT 360 exercise to ensure long term success. Gamification or the application of game psychology and game dynamics, to non-game situations is potentially powerful when applied to meaningful touch points in your employee interactions.

I have been using game thinking and psychology for nearly twenty years, yet it was only about ten years ago that I discover there was an actual term for it. I grew up in a sports oriented family; my dad was a sports journalist and my mum a graphic designer, so to connect those two strong influences wasn't too hard. I always used sports analogies, and since I was eight, I designed crosswords. I always performed quite well in school, because I set myself gamified goals and rewards. I had all sorts of trackers and thermometers on my wall to publicly record when tasks were completed and goals were achieved, or in notebooks if I wanted to keep them secret.

My first bicycle was bought with the pocket money I saved. Every weekend, without fail, we counted how much was in my piggybank and calculated how much more I needed to save. This information went on to my bike saving tracker chart. For more money, I did odd chores like washing the car and negotiated additional rewards towards my bicycle. Even visitors received the same persistent approach from me. When I had saved over half of the bike fund in cash, I used coupons, saved from a catalogue store to make up the difference, and that's how I bought my bicycle, aged eight. I was mega proud to have earned that bike. It wasn't quite a BMX, but it looked like it could withstand a few tricks and stunts. In any case it provided a good few years of fun.

The saving and tracking process taught me that game mechanics work for me. Later on in my career, specifically in change management and executive coaching, I applied similar techniques, but tailored them to suit the individual or team I was working with. I remember one particular change management project where there was potential for a team to walk out on strike over working conditions and differing pay structures. I approached the team manager and said "If we bring the team together, and organise a night out to let off steam, we may get the guys back on board.". It worked; the team got a chance to air their thoughts in an informal setting, as well as enjoy some fun together. This made a big difference to their performance and commitment for the next few weeks.

When people start to complain and want to tell you what could be better, it's a good idea to listen, specifically listen for potentially constructive feedback, and don't overlook the emotion behind the message either. In some organisations criticism is seen as a way of undermining management, whilst that may be true, more often it comes from a team or individual getting up the courage to speak up and let you know that they care very much about the situation and want to improve it.

In my change management work I actively invited these types of conversation, as well as using feedback to clarify what I thought I was hearing, was correct. We would then agree constructive goals to improve the situation, and the person in question often had key responsibilities for delivering that change. To create a positive atmosphere, I also had celebration of achievement in mind. So my experience is that listening, and taking on board what could be done better, has produced a good return on my time investment. Now I also pay attention to the emotion driving this feedback; by showing I care means both parties are invested in making change work. So that's an easy to identify with illustration of how gamification and human centric design thinking works for me and I know it will work for you too.

Often when I start speaking about gamification people imagine fancy game scenarios and expensive tracking tools. For years I managed to do it without a hint of technology in sight, now that technological tools are readily available it would be silly not to use them, but it still doesn't have to be costly.

The key to making gamification design a successful tool for change management and performance management work is to understand the emotions and profiles of your target audience, which is either your employee or your customer. Therefore, it is probably no surprise to you that I start all my gamification design with in-depth user research. I want to engage in that conversation of how things are working from the employee or customer perspective, so I encourage clients to do this by interviewing of individuals and working with focus groups on a specific topic (typically the business process you are intending to improve), not forgetting useful feedback obtained from targeted questionnaires. The user research phase is vitally important in order to get your gamification design right. In my experience, failure rates will be higher when you skip this step. For business start-ups that want advice about gamifying apps, I usually ask them to describe their target audience; unfortunately, most of them have no idea how to answer, which in my view makes gamification impossible.

Competency personality profiles created during the

recruitment process, customer feedback and employee engagement statistics, google analytics for marketing, all help organisations to identify key business processes that are broken; typically, these are the areas that result highly on a complaints index and low on in terms of satisfaction. This information provides an organisation with an indication or whether or not their gamification design process will result in lasting change, or needs improving in general.

User research provides a clearer picture of the types of people you want to target. In terms of user experience design, you basically want to build a persona. This personal profile is useful for gamification design because it includes a vast amount of information about what motivates the individual, their habits, what troubles them, what games they play, what they enjoy, how they experience fun and achievement. Additionally, it includes regular things such as why they engage with a certain process, what their objectives are, what their habits are, where their regular environments are, where they tend to socialise, what they read, preferences on social media channels et cetera. You need to be able name them, picture them and even create a storyboard about your target. Many organisations will have more than one persona, so know the two or three and design your gamification strategy for them.

We also explore how each persona relates to motivation. Each user persona typically has a particular motivational driver. For example, if I'm a high achiever, I tend to want to remain a high achiever, and I tend not to tolerate people who do not pull their weight. If I need to change the focus on where my achievement goes, that's okay, I just need to know that I can still achieve. So if I go from a results orientated hard working mentality, to a loose, but exuberant, feel good friendly type of structure, the high achievers may no longer feel like they're effective anymore. Obviously a change of that nature may not be desirable in business, just know that change tends to have consequences for the environment, culture and its people. A catch all strategy will not be the most efficient for results, however noble it may be to try and create one.

From a gamification strategy perspective, we focus on designing the game around the type of persona and behaviour you want to encourage more of. We look for things what will support your new vision and assist you in creating the game plot to help make it work. Straight after the user persona has been clarified, we look at the business objectives to explore how they match in relation to your new vision. Each business objective then becomes a measurable, quantifiable KPI. We have often also included a happiness index as a softer measure while taking a helicopter view of the sentiment of a company.

Then we get busy designing the game.

Where possible, I get the crowd to design the game with me in design thinking workshops by creating smaller mixed function teams (15-20 people). In each workshop, one key objective is addressed. For example, it could be how to improve the recruitment process, or how to make performance management personally valuable. We then address which processes need to be changed and how to do it; basically, we consider everything, including how to have the most fun achieving it.

I ask participants to look at each process in four stages:
1.   How will we attract people to engage with this new or

improved process?

2. What are the first steps they take?

3. How will we engage them in the long run?

4. What is the end-game or an infinite loop back to the start?

The attraction phase looks at how people will find out about your new process, is it publicised or will it just be rolled out. Will participation be voluntary, or will everyone be signed up without an opt-out. I personally prefer voluntary approaches and letting the new way of working do the talking, however, this is not always practical for each process.

The engagement phase needs to look at the first few steps people will take in your new or improved way of working. When there are new systems to contend with, you may need to include tutorials, or glowing choices as game mechanics to make the process work and to allow users to become efficient quickly. In most games this is also where quick wins and early rewards come into play, so we discuss what these could be.

The nurturing phase is where we spend more time than the previous phases, because we are talking about longer term engagement, multiple potential game mechanics, and communication initiatives to keep people working with the new process. It looks at the use of levels and game playing that could enhance the users experience and outcomes.

The end game is often an easy question to answer, the process starts over at the end of a given time period or a particular milestone. Just like in sports tournament, you have a winner and then next year you start the process all over again. Or you may have an infinite game system where the strategy just carries on. Even in these infinite games, we always recommend having a success zone to be achieved in a given time period such as a minimum number of points accumulated for tasks, this gives an indication on what is considered good, and what is below par.

For these gamification design workshops, I usually bring along a few sets of gamification cards with game mechanics on them to get the conversations started. We split the group into teams of five and each come ups with an approach for each phase. In this way we tend to generate more ideas than in one big group. The teams then present back their ideas, following which, we reward individuals the voting power to pick their top *must haves* across each phase. This gives us an indication of what could be perceived of highest importance.

Then we either go to implementation if a gamification platform has been chosen, or we build a concept pilot to test what was suggested has been interpreted correctly, as well as check how it could look on existing systems in the organisation. In most cases this will lead to minor tweaks and confirmation of the overall concept. The gamification design documentation is where all the interactions and thinking is captured and will remain a reference point for future development. It is also the starting point for a platform provider to make it come to live.

Design and implementation follows one another rather swiftly. You're building expectation, you're building momentum. If you start something and you raise an expectation by inviting people to give input, then people will naturally want to see something happen as a result. The concept pilot will give them some idea, but it's the actual roll out that people are holding out for. Where possible, we implement small things straight away, and we keep changing and tweaking and developing it further from there.

Iterations are normal and key in gamification; you continue to make your game better based on feedback. All big game corporations will have strong business analytics departments. They know exactly where people are dropping out, which levels they find hard. Even that's not so hard to measure with today's feedback on sites like YouTube. People are constantly showing us how they've actually managed to get through a specific "hard" level. For every popular game you will have people creating game hacks such as help sheets or YouTube tutorial videos to help others move forward too. Now imagine this level of interest, support and feedback happening in your working environment.

I spoke at one point to one of the business intelligence people at *King*; they produce a lot of the casual games like *Candy Crush* and *Candy Soda Saga*. This is now our conversation played out:

King "Oh, are you playing Candy Crush"?

Me "Yeah, absolutely. I'm at this level".

King "Wow, you're one of our 0.01 percent of people that actually go that far and play that long".

Me (laughing) "Wow, that's motivational".

King "Yeah, that's scary, because you're the guys that we just can't control - I bet you never paid for a thing, either".

Me "No".

King "Yeah, we don't write games for you anymore".

It was funny how he knew that. It's also funny when I work with an organisation, and we're looking at behaviour change, just how few of them are tracking what they're doing, how few of them know exactly where the change has actually taken place, or not. I strongly urge that during the implementation stage of your game design, you look at ways of measuring:

a)   How you made it from where you were to where you are now?

b)   How will you know that you succeeded?

There will be a lot of questions along this line.

Some energy into measuring how they made it from A to B as well as how will they know when they've arrived at where they want to be? There will be a lot more questions along this line.

A big part of this process is, once you've got all your systems are in place, all your games are in place, and your vision is in place, you let your employees get on with it. This is probably the hardest part for most traditional managers, including people that have been trained in traditional leadership skills. Let them self-support, let them rank and vote, let them use the feedback loops that you have built into your system, be tolerant, not everything will work first time.   You may sometimes have to do iterations and say "Okay, this approach didn't work, how can we tweak it that maybe next time, it does work"? Always be constructive and welcome feedback and celebrate and learn from failures. To put it in Einstein's words is "I found another way that didn't work". Was he saying he failed, no! He was simply saying he found another way that didn't work.

Traditional companies have in the main considered firing anyone who did wrong. Maybe that's not the best approach, especially considering what we have learnt from mistakes. Instead, we need to look at *why* things go wrong, and how we can rectify them. Maybe they were onto something, or maybe they did do something that took it too far, maybe there is just one element, or tweak that is needed in order to fix what's missing - that's a lot of maybes, but you get the drift, we need a different approach to thinking though different issues.

One approach to thinking differently is when you rely on the crowd to self-correct, and that when they have good data, dashboards, data feeds and data analyses, they will be able to make better decisions. For example, if a campaign is going south and it is not exactly delivering what was expected, ask them "How can it be changed to save it? How could you support them? Sometimes, that could be the best response.

The way I look at it, in today's world, we have total access to lots of analysis. The types of dashboards I love are those that are shown after the world's economic forum in Switzerland, which you can find on https://www.weflive.com. They're the Twitter feeds, the social media sites, and the sentiment tracking of everything that's happening. If you use internal social media combined with internal social network, then you can replicate exactly this within your organisation, including exactly this type of tracking to capture who's saying what about this, what your customers are experiencing, what's happening inside, what's happening outside and so forth.

Have one ear on both sides of the equation and look at those types of bubbles. I think it will give you a real impression of the sentiments of the people inside your organisation, but make your dashboard visible to all. That will also show people that you're being transparent about everything that your people are doing, which is beneficial for instigating discussion, adjusting strategy and potentially pre-empting problems, before they become so large they need to be addressed formally.

This is my gamification design approach to tapping into the crowd. Giving them the tools to do what they need to do in order to be the best possible versions of them-self.

Let's look now to our next chapter and the role of the manager and the employee, and how gamification actually makes things happen, including, how it plays out in the life cycle of an employee.

CHAPTER EIGHT
TAPPING INTO THE CROWD
ALL ALONG THE EMPLOYEE LIFECYCLE

Tapping into the crowd

In previous chapters, we explored how crowdsourcing and gamification can make a huge difference in your strategy implementations. It doesn't have to end here though; we see it as an opportunity to positively influence the whole of the operational side of the business. In fact, we can even explore gamification and crowdsourcing throughout an employee lifecycle. I see the employee lifecycle starting with an employer's branding, followed by what happens during recruitment, on-boarding, training, performance management, promotions, rotations, career path planning and alumni networks. Each process has what we call in experience design terms *meaningful touchpoints*, which are basically points you can impress, or distress as an organisation, and at which point you also have the chance to win employee buy-in.

Both gamification and crowdsourcing tap into the power of intrinsic motivation. This provides an inner driving force that actively encourages people to shine and voluntarily release their inner strengths. Intrinsic motivation is an enabler; it helps people to do what they want to do, to the best of their ability, following which, gamification provides them the feedback tool, allowing them to do that to an even greater extent.

Employer branding

In order to make *tapping into the crowd* a way of life in your organisation, you need to look at the narrative and messaging that you are sending out into the market with your employer branding efforts. You want to share stories about how you do business, why it works, and who it works for. You could have employer branding events where you invite potential employees to experience a day in the life of your organisation. Ask them to actively engage in what is important to them as a potential employee, be they sales, engineering or finance. Ask what they want to know then find a way to provide them with the information. In my view this is a reciprocal process for a free day trial that ends with you getting feedback in return.

Employer branding starts long before someone is looking for a job in your organisation. Just think about all the brands you engage with on a daily basis and upon which you have developed an opinion, whether intended or not.

Creating curiosity and a positive sentiment towards your brand, as well as the potential of wanting to belong to a company like yours, should be the main purpose of employer branding. When it comes to branding, most companies think big budget, which can be true if it means getting external public relations involved. However, in the spirit of crowdsourcing, I would challenge you to take this effort in a more creative direction. Ask your employees to contribute with smart phone images, audio and video stories all with a dedicated hashtag on social media. Pick one or two relevant platforms, set a few guidelines, and then let your people get creative.

Logistics giant *Maersk*, used this approach to shed light on the fact that they are not just a logistics company, but they also have an oil and gas division. The differentiators they chose to focus on were innovation and it being a great place to work. They actively wanted to portray the options of a career on their platforms, so they asked employees to help them by posting stories of what life is like on an oil rig with video messages on their Facebook page. They didn't set many rules, they let people decide what was ok to share, which they admitted was a risk, but they also knew they could trust their people. In fact, one of the oil rig chefs became a mini celebrity; people actually wanted to see his *day in the life* clips, which developed a great following. Working in a confined space, with limited resources, takes creativity and the chef shared his recipes, challenges and fun. It inspired people and it's an entertaining way of expressing what reality is like while engaging with followers. This in my view is how to tap into your crowd for employer branding, nothing staged or edited, just the reality of people doing their daily thing.

In conjunction with this campaign, the company went one step further into the future, and created a full-blown game aimed at teenagers in school. It has a big budget game production called *Quest for Oil* (http://www.maersk.com/en/hardware/quest-for-oil) with an educational element to it; it teaches about the geography of oil drilling, and the different conditions that could be encountered based on location. The strategy is aimed at opening the eyes of 14-16 year olds to raise awareness of the career paths open for some of them. They also work closely with schools to give a true educational value to this material.

Generation Y is still active on all social media platforms, so all social is good, and for generation Z we said *Instagram, Snapchat, Pinterest, YouTube* are favoured for thinking images and thinking movies. The *day in the life* approach can work across both generations quite happily because games are of big interest for both these age groups, so the dual approach from *Maersk* will definitely pay off for a long term strategy. Then again, the nature of brand building tends to be more strategic and long term in any case.

Recruitment

Tapping into the crowd from a recruitment perspective with gamification built in at its core is known as a hackathon. A hackathon can be explained *as a quest to resolve a specific problem chosen by you to test the skills and creativity of the people invited to take part in them.* Hackathons have been used by IT companies where a difficult problem is presented and only those coders and developers who can come up with a good solution are invited for further interviews. These days we see hackathons appear more frequently, even in non-technical fields, where potential recruits are put through a series of challenges to test their competencies, resilience, and response to ambiguous or difficult situations. It can be set as an individual or a group challenge with hiring team members and managers even taking part.

The benefits of using this approach to recruitment are that you receive true feedback about the ability and working style of an individual, together with the potential of seeing them already as a colleague. Organisations such as *Facebook, IBM* and *Google* are some of the well-known users of this technique for both innovation, as well as recruitment purposes.

The more lifelike you make the challenge, the better the outcome for the individual who is assessing working for you, and you the employer in evaluating them. Again, this approach does not take huge capital investment, nor involves being online. A hackathon requires a location, a facilitator, a problem which can be split into multiple facets, which requires participants and evaluation standards.

For companies looking to take this kind of challenge online, a good example comes from *PWC* in Hungary, they wanted to reach university graduates of non-financial degree programs. They knew these students could make great employees, but they typically didn't apply through the traditional channels. So, they set up *Multipoly,* which was an online replica of their building, and invited targeted *Facebook* users to come and play. They were given a variety of tests to see what their skills and interests were. Tasks were set and completion of a quest received feedback from job coaches. Competency testing and real job challenges were at the core of this exercise as well as feedback.

A number of online tools have entered the market allowing you to create this style of recruitment quest, the ones we recommend include *Games for Business,* who also custom built the *Multipoly* example and have since built an engagement engine for HR, and then *Hackerrank,* which allows you to set mainly IT related hack challenges. One tool that especially impressed me, but is more game based, rather than crowdsourced or gamified is *Pymetrics.* It blends mini-games, an algorithm, neuroscience and job matches based on the values and potential you are seeking.

The other side of the recruitment process where I believe your internal crowd of employees can help is with referrals for specific job openings. Some companies have used this technique to great effect, by first of all notifying employees about career opportunities and rewarding them when they recommend a suitable candidate. Some companies reward the referring employee upon hiring; some after the probation period has successfully been completed, while others reward both the new hire and the referring employee. There is no one best reward system, but it is important to give value to the process. Most employees will only refer a person they see as suitable, because they know their company, and they also realise that bad referrals could reflect badly on them.

Where gamification in the recruitment process can make a difference is in the feedback process. Most candidates, especially when they have reached interview stage, require feedback about whether they are progressing or not. I recommend feeding back two things a candidate showcased well, as well as two areas for improvement, ready for the next interview as a useful personalised form of feedback. I know from personal experience, the vast amount of companies do not even give candidates the courtesy of a 'Thank you for applying, we don't have an appropriate vacancy', or 'We will keep your CV on file' type of response.

When it comes to interviews, both parties have a vested interest, and it is in my view only natural to then expect feedback one way or another. The companies that are doing this well are adding for example, a dashboard for the candidate to see how far they have come in the process, how many more steps they have to complete, and whether they have a green light to progress or not. So, a simple progress bar with traffic lights and an optional button for the candidate to request feedback, which triggers an email to the interviewer requesting feedback. A timeframe for this button to remain live is also acceptable, because when interviewing candidates consecutively, the memory fades, alternatively, make it standard practise to give candidates immediate feedback. Even when being turned down in the process, feedback could make the process worthwhile for the candidate, because when a rejected is carried out gracefully, the perception of the company remains intact. The flipside is, if this process is handled badly, it's a waste of all the previous investment in both employer branding and the recruitment process.

On-boarding

When you organise a group of new hires to start together, you immediately create a sense of camaraderie, which will help them throughout their career with your organisation. The shared experience of the unknown is one people remember and it creates informal networks. It doesn't matter if they work in the same team or not, just having a fellow new hire to speak to allows new hires to make friends early on.

If group starts are not an option, then the process of on-boarding could still be fun and engaging. In fact, this process can even be gamified for both the hiring manager, as well as the new starter. For the manager quest, you want to make sure they have everything ready to welcome their new team member. Not every manager will hire new team members on a regular basis, so even if they do a simple reminder system to make sure the processes are completed, it will work well. I worked on a project where we actually had a traffic light system for managers and teams that were welcoming a new hire, it showcased how well they were already progressing. Green was a welcome light for new starters. Yellow or amber lights meant they were getting to a good place and again it included the next steps to take and finally, a red traffic light meant they weren't ready at all and it indicated the steps yet to be completed. The traffic light system was built on the existing process that needed to be completed for security logins, access, seating, equipment, initial training and meeting and greeting key people.

Most frequently, on-boarding quests are aimed at the new

hire and often run by HR or the manager, often the reality is a new person arrives in chaos and lands in the deep end. Even if your organisation has carried out great efforts on employer branding and recruitment, missing this step can immediately lose your credibility with new people. When hiring new candidates, a failure to welcome them properly could end up as their creative expression on social media. Because this process is fully under your control, it would be silly to miss out on an opportunity to impress and create further loyalty.

A great example of gamified on-boarding comes from *KLM*. Even the design process to come up with their on-boarding strategy was innovative. They invited a number of providers to come and share their vision. They shared how they wanted it to be perceived, what the problems were, and they asked different providers to come up with solutions. They were given access to decision makers in each of the teams and given the remit to design a prototype of an application.

What they chose as their winner was an application where a new starter receives a suitcase, which perfectly suited the airline. Every day the new hire received one or more quests to fulfil that day, ranging from having to go and collect their swipe card, to meeting key people, to getting access codes for all the various software that they needed to use.

They put the onus on both the manager to prepare whatever was relevant into the app for the individual, and the individual to self-organise, because *KLM* saw independence and initiative as key skills to success in their organisation. Their apps also had funny things in it such as "Find your way to the loo", or "Find your way to building X you're expected there at such a time". Individuals were given the resources in their app to do what they needed to do, but it depended on them to succeed. At each stage feedback was provided which then unlocked new steps.

The main aim for on-boarding is to make the person feel like they have made the right decision by coming to work for you in your team and organisation. Nobody enjoys being the new kid in an unknown environment, especially when everyone else seems to know how things work, so making this process smoother is an illustration of how it can be fun, and adapted to fit your culture while giving individuals what they need to succeed.

Culture and performance

Once a new hire has found their way, they will learn the vast majority of the culture on the ground by interacting with team members, managers and colleagues further afield. Company culture is the glue that holds the organisation together. Culture is built on rituals, stories, events, it comes from celebrating achievement, learning from failure, creating a culture where it is acceptable to fail and acceptable to be creative and innovate. When you look at the companies who feature in the lists of great places to work at, they have a number of things in common, namely, they have good people policies, a strong culture, with room to be innovative and creative, typically, they are also active in offering well-being benefits, activities and areas.

I recommend starting out with creating an infrastructure by design, one that underpins your cultural values. When your work environment reflects what the company stands for it often creates that feeling for people too. It is reflected in the colours, the work areas, maybe fun break-outs, resting areas, quiet zones, meeting spaces all the way to comfortable seating and working desks. In terms of softer infrastructure, you are looking at creating benefit packages that reflect the company culture, and support individuality with a range of choices in your local community. Use crowdsourced ideas from your existing employees to draft up plans for office space as well as benefit packages.

Celebrating success is probably the easiest element to put into place, but it's also an area many businesses and their management teams are reluctant to do, possibly out of fear around setting expectations. The thing is by celebrating what truly matters and raising the bar on a regular basis you also create a culture of excellence. However, if you celebrate mediocrity and keep expectations the same, you will stagnate, even go backwards. If this is where you need to start, fine, but aim to raise the bar to whatever a good standard looks like.

What I find in my work with large organisations is that many employees do not understand what good looks like in their role, or even how to deliver it. In those instances, I suggest setting goals or objectives, with tangible results that indicate a success zone, one where people receive feedback that they are delivering value on an every daily basis. One of the tools we offer is *MyObjectives,* software that facilitates the process of showing people what their contribution is against goals, and how well they are performing on a regular basis.

I often have the discussion with HR directors on how they gather a massive amount of information on individuals working for their company, yet only a limited amount of it is used to create a positive sentiment. For example, attendance data can easily be part of a daily login message to state to the individual that they have a 100% unbroken attendance record, and still take x amount of days holidays this year. It promotes both attendance as well as taking breaks.

Another application I see easily adapted to employee feedback is the customer service measurement tap board with a happy, neutral and unhappy face as you leave a store or a security area in the airport. It doesn't need to be individualised, it just gives you trends of how the mood is in the organisation. The same with listening to social media about your company with a correlation back to the commentary that comes from customers and another from employees. I think it is essential management intelligence and totally possible with today's technology. Feedback as they say "Is the breakfast of champions"; in order to improve and become better, feedback is a great teacher.

In terms of management and leadership, dashboards like *MyObjectives* or *Betterworks*, ensure the vision and overall corporate goals are translated into departmental, team and individual goals. They create a level of transparency as well as the requirement to step up and take responsibility in each role. Most game players are used to a *Heads Up Display*, meaning the number that you see at the top of each game telling you how many lives you have, and how far up the levels you are. This kind of feedback is what people are increasingly looking for. You can in fun ways give them points towards achievement, but also scores for flagging trouble point or potential bottle necks, scores for progress, and voting rights. Give employees as much input where possible, both positive and negative.

The two-way feedback will create a sense of real ownership, but equally with ownership comes responsibility which allows them to make decisions and to self-manage in an educated way. If I'm a sales person and I have feedback on how many customers we actually successfully closed deals with, how many potential leads there are, and how market sentiment is towards us, I have useful feedback which can influence my actions. If for example, I'm a call centre agent and I see there are twenty people in a queue, I know that my speed of working through calls might need to pick up. I can improve my skills with showing how my success rate is. It's giving people the chance to measure themselves, and to make informed decisions on behalf of the company.

If a dashboard shows you feedback from the market, or from employees that something's not quite working, it provides you with an opportunity to crowd resolve the situation. You can ask "What could we do differently? What can we learn and improve from this situation? Where can we go from here? Who else needs to be involved? Are just some of the questions to ask. Even on projects or interactions that have worked well so far, there is still an opportunity to learn and improve. Great organisations learn from both success and failure and they allow for their teams to reflect on what can be done better next time. What is critical as a manager is to showcase your flexibility and facilitate this kind of discussion. Show your team that you've noticed, show them that you actually respect where they are and say "Look it's okay, let's think and talk it through and go from there". Nothing, unless there's been some criminal damage done or something illegal has happened, should be a complete show stopper. In business it is normal to live and learn, in game terms it means one life is over, and now you start with life two. In most games you get five lives, then twenty minutes later it refreshes again.

Tapping into the crowd

Most of our careers are built up from learning points; if you want to build that kind of learning culture, you have to be the one supporting it. You have to be the one spotting it from the data, inquiring what was happening and facilitating the support. If it means everybody needs to take a timeout, that's okay too. In games you do have that period where you cannot play. If that means you have to bench your players for a few days to think something through, that's okay because sometimes, downtime gives you exactly what's needed to come back with fresh eyes and fresh input. I always use the game analogy because it's a powerful one. I've worked with it all my life, it works for me and my decision making, it works in everything I do.

I encourage you to find the game that best reflects your business and industry and where possible using the game analogy above. Start by asking a question like: "Where is the game in what we already do that we could build on"? Remember, most failures are not fatal. For most of us, failure is a dent in our egos, or a dent in our enthusiasm, but it doesn't mean we can't pick something back up and start over. Champions have learned from failing, adjusting, and getting better, training harder and coming back. Apply that analogy, because it's something that you as a company decision maker can set and encourage and influence. Pick your game, make it companywide, make it fun, and encourage your team to share their stories, the rituals, show off the rituals and remember to lead by example.

Learning and development

As part of the learning and development function, both crowdsourcing content, and gamification are proving to be a winning combination for my clients. This year alone every single learning related gamification project included the option to self-generate learning tracks and content tracks with the requirement of measuring progress and feedback on performance as a key ingredient. None of these projects were built without end-user feedback. Each and every one of our clients had their employees asking for the opportunity to share, collaborate and experience some fun as a way to learning and achieving more.

Most generations X, Y and Z are so internet savvy, their first instinct is to carry out a google search or a search in the company learning catalogue, whenever they are stuck for ways of doing something. The role of learning and development is changing, it is becoming more a curator style function, rather than the traditional one as provide by many companies. So consider providing employees with access to external tools that are pre-approved trusted resources. Reward them for continuous upgrading their skills. Reward them with motivational tracking of their learning efforts. Make it meaningful and relevant so that it matters to them. Allow and encourage employees to continually improve and sponsor certifications.

If you want the crowd to take part in your learning, you need to make it as relevant to them as possible. Be open for them to share what else they need, what else they want, what else is missing and encourage them to help you fill that gap that they claim is there. I encourage learning teams to set up content leader boards based on the rating given by learners for each piece of learning they took on board. This provides you with feedback about what to invest more of as well as what to let go of. I say gamification will do a lot for an improved learning experience, which is a topic for another book, but suffice to say, as far as tapping into the crowd goes;

ensure your employees know how much you value the knowledge they arrive with, and how much it means to you for them to constantly be developing and improving their skills. It is a win-win for both parties, one that usually fosters a more creative workforce, because you not only allow, but encourage them to explore their curiosity to all new areas of work and beyond.

Community spirit

When people feel they belong in an organisation where they can do their best work, feel valued for it and be amongst like-minded individuals, the chances of them being engaged and willing to go the extra mile increase dramatically. Creating a community spirit in a global organisation is more challenging than in a smaller local one, yet it is still possible. International meet and greet sessions are great, but equally expensive, so not readily available for every budget.

However, this issue was overcome by one multinational because of an employee well-being initiative that created a fabulous community spirit even if there was a competitive spirit that travelled with it at the same time. Employees were divided into random international teams and asked to meet once a week online to discuss what they had done to look after their health and well-being that week. In the intermittent days they used the internal social network to keep each other motivated and updated. Each team scored when all the team members logged evidence of positive action either in the shape of *Fitbit* print outs, logged walks, images with time stamps etc. What happened was that whilst this campaign ran over 6 weeks, people established fun human relationships with colleagues in offices further afield; hence when they had projects to complete and didn't know who to speak to, they turned to their well-being team members for help. Because people generally felt better, overall productivity of the company went up, which was measured in project completions and resulted in a surprise bonus that this challenge wasn't intended to deliver on. Challenges like these do not require more than a concerted effort of management teams and some fancy email work with one leader board to make something fresh and fun happen.

Alumni communities

A sense of belonging can remain long after a project finishes, even when someone leaves there still remains a sense of community for the people inside, but also an exit or alumni community - for organisations that retain their links. For example, most ex Googlers are called ex Googlers and they will say that for years after, these individuals will often be re-hired, or have the projects sponsored in new organisations. Some organisations make it an active strategy to place their former employees in key positions at organisations they want to do business with. Many companies keep in touch with ex-employees because they're still a valuable resource of feedback, and you can both say things you didn't say when they were working together, plus you could also find out how the market is affecting the company or spot other opportunities that you can't see if you're only receiving feedback from the inside. So keeping close ties with ex-employees and allowing them to meet up with your team on a regular basis, maybe even on your premises, at your invite with you there as a CEO will help you gain valuable contributions.

Communication is the glue that makes it stick together

Communication is what pulls all of this together; it's continuous communication from and about projects that are working well, which are motivational, and of course the bloopers and outtakes are the funny one recounted years later, all of which are the stories that shape a company.

If I look into the future with the potential for technology and communication to converge, imagine where the manager pops up as a hologram, and gives you a big cheer because you did something well. That can be instigated by the click of a button. Or a *Pokemon Go* style scan function that allows you to open a personal training session, or reminder on how to use certain tools with sticker codes on them and learning hiding behind them. Imagine a boost or pep-talk on demand through the push of a button, or a senior manager coming over to genuinely chat with the team and spur things forward as a coach who wants the best for all his players in the company.

Technology is an enabler for the world we live in today, and crowdsourcing has become a major influence in how decisions are being made, including how business is being conducted. Human connections will continue to thrive and it is that authentic pat on the back or truly listening ear that will bring motivation from the inside out. It is about digital, human and behavioural communication coming together to create the best possible environment for all of us to thrive in.

Conclusion

The power of the crowd is coming towards us whether we like it or not. New generations mean the workforce's attitudes are constantly changing, and the only way to close the gap in employee disengagement and raise the bar towards employee delight, is to build on the amazing power that resides inside the people - inside your organisation.

Gamification and crowdsourcing are two powerful resources currently available that can support you achieve this mission. With younger generations coming into the workplace absolute natives to these approaches, it would be an oversight not to engage in some of these proven techniques. So, I strongly urge you to switch on that super power, switch on that extra muscle booster living inside your own employees, because I believe that every human being, with the exception of a tiny minority, actually want to be proud of their contribution and do a good days work, so creating an environment of employee delight is something worth striving for.

I've given you plenty of food for thought, which I hope will inspire you to take new action. I would love to hear about your successes or even help you achieve them.

Thank you for reading and please share socially what you doing to make things happen to create employee delight in your organisation.

If you need help in making this all happen we are obviously always happy to support you in this process. For more information, you can contact us on www.gamificationnation.com or fun@gamificationnation.com. An Coppens can be found on all social media including the new ones. We're never hard to find or ask a question from.

ABOUT THE AUTHOR
AN COPPENS

An Coppens is an award winning entrepreneur and chief game changer at Gamification Nation Ltd. She is considered an expert in the area of gamification for employee and learner engagement.

Gamification Nation Ltd, which offers gamification design solutions and an online gamification community. The company is based in London and serving clients worldwide from well-known brands to smaller product focused SME's.

Her solutions are designed to encourage winning behaviours and improve business results in the areas of sales, marketing, HR, learning and productivity. In 2016 she was recognized at the World HRD congress in Mumbai as a HR tech visionary.

Projects she has worked on included reviewing onboarding of sales staff and their recognition, assisting managers with getting ready for new hires, website gamification, gamification of an in-house learning curriculum, membership site gamification, etc.

Increasing engagement is always our key focus.

She is an award winning business coach, speaker, learning & development professional and author. She is a prolific blogger on gamification through www.gamificationnation.com and tweets under her Twitter alter ego @GamificationNat. Her 3rd book called "Gamification in Business" is available for download from http://bookboon.com/en/gamification-in-business-ebook.

In her career An has worked in learning and development and change management roles for Modern Times Group, Xigma Management Consultants, Philips Electronics and Arthur Andersen Business Consulting. She was a guest expert on the TV show "How long will you live" for RTE in Ireland. For 10 years An ran a successful business coaching practice in Cork, Ireland with B/Right Business Coaching. She holds a BA (Hon) in International Marketing and languages from Dublin City University and an MBA from the Open University Business School in the UK. She holds a gamification master qualification from the Engagement Alliance and has completed a number of online gamification courses.

www.gamificationnation.com
@GamificationNat

GLOSSARY

Gamification: Applying game psychology, game design and mechanics to non-game situations such as business performance, productivity, HR, etc.

Hack-a- ton: A term derived from IT hacking, which was originally used to hack or break into a system and disrupt it. Now it is the common term used to brainstorm and generate ideas to disrupt old processes and come up with new innovations in relation to a common problem. The participants for a hack-a- ton are often selected from a variety of backgrounds to have multiple different perspectives and ideas.

Level-up: to move up a level, often used in games when a player completes one level and moves on to another. In business it would mean to achieve the next level skillset or managerial positioning.

Heads Up Display: also known as HUD is the scoreboard for online games, it includes information on points earned, lives left, time, etc. depending on what elements of scoring are essential to win in a game.

Flatarchies: no hierarchy, everyone is in charge of their own role and takes responsibility to get the job done.

RESOURCES

Chapter 1: crowd sourcing

Global crowdsourcing stats: http://eyeka.pr.co/99215-eyeka-releases-the-state-of-crowdsourcing-in-2015-trend-report

http://www.crowdsourcing.org/editorial/global-crowdfunding-market-to-reach-344b-in-2015-predicts-massolutions-2015cf-industry-report/45376

Book Reality is broken – Jane McGonigal

Ted Talk of Jane

Book Maverick – Ricardo Semler

Ted Talk of Ricardo

5 P's OF THE
CROWD ECONOMY

BROUGHT TO YOU BY CSW² & CROWDSOURCING WEEK

PEOPLE   PURPOSE   PARTICIPATION   PLATFORM   PRODUCTIVITY

Empowering, disruption, and human-centric   Creates meaningful experiences   Emphasis on co-creation and shared value   Medium to interact and drive results   Faster, cheaper, more efficient processes

Chapter 2 – Employee engagement

http://home.southernct.edu/~pager1/gallup.htm

http://www.gallup.com/businessjournal/182321/employees-lot-managers.aspx?g_source=position1&g_medium=related&g_campaign=tiles

Chapter 3 – strategy

1. People as strategic competitive advantage
   a. Strategy models
   b. Competition and competitive advantage
   c. From driving forces to value based working (value chain, based leadership – Porter/Kotter, etc.
   d. Game theory
   e. Internal resource management: Semler/ Porter – disrupting hierarchies
   f. Collaboration, self-empowerment and evolving leaders
   g. Book refs: Maverick – Semler and Porter multiple books

Supporting material from chapter: Book, videos, images, slideshares etc.

John Kotter – Our iceberg is melting

John Kotter – 8 step process to leading change http://www.kotterinternational.com/8-steps-process-for-leading-change/

Tapping into the crowd

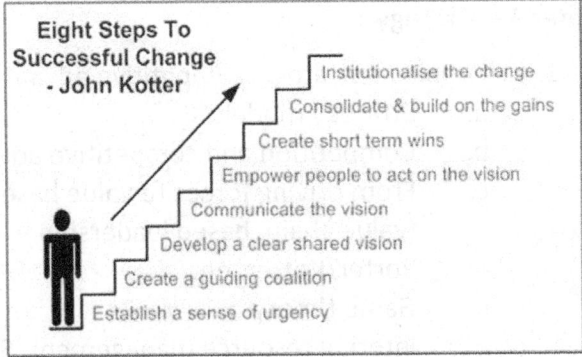

http://www.slideshare.net/ToeyNumber10/our-iceberg-is-melting-presentation/37-
Like other good stories you

Ricardo Semler – Maverick

https://www.ted.com/talks/ricardo_semler_radical_wisdom_for_a_company_a_school_a_life?language=en

Ken Blanchard – High Five

Tom Peters – Re-imagine
https://www.youtube.com/watch?v=NWO2mjp5Hsg

Michael Porter - Competitive Strategy: Techniques for Analyzing Industries and Competitors

Five forces model

Chapter 4 – the changing nature of the workforce and work place

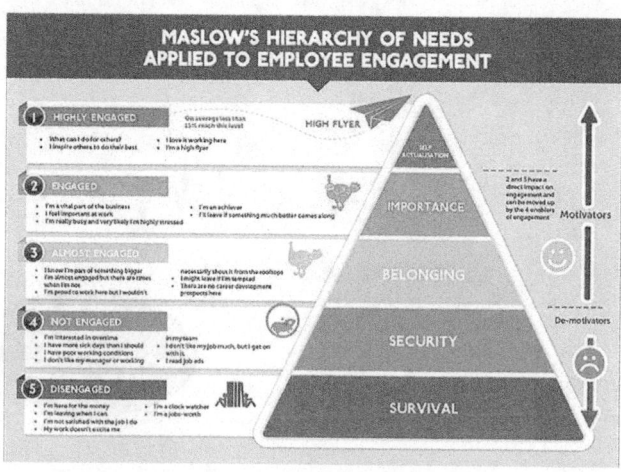

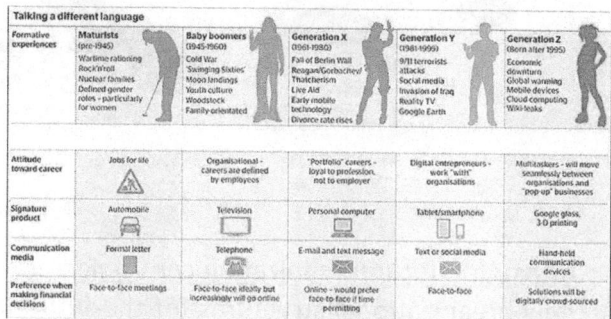

http://sproutsocial.com/insights/gen-z-vs-gen-y/

http://www.slideshare.net/sparksandhoney/generatio
n-z-final-june-17

http://www.huffingtonpost.com/tim-
elmore/contrasting-generation-y-_b_5679434.html

Think Malala / Ted talk about hack schooling / what
adults can learn from children

Chapter 5 – organisational structures

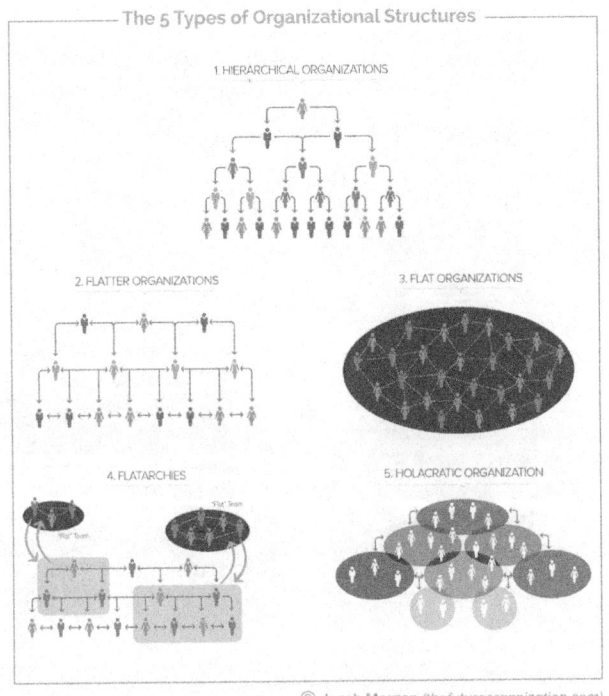

© Jacob Morgan *(thefutureorganization.com)*

https://thefutureorganization.com/holacracy-and-new-organizational-structures-for-the-future-of-work/

https://youtu.be/tJxfJGo-vkI

http://www.holacracy.org/how-it-works/

Further resources:

Gamified recruitment

Heineken the candidate
https://www.youtube.com/watch?v=a9JLJ4cm3W8

ABOUT
PENCRAFT BOOKS, LLC

At PenCraft Books (PCB) we know what it's like to have a dream of being a published author. Individually, we have been through the publishing process. It isn't easy and the entire process from writing to having books sold requires a huge learning curve.

At PCB we're committed to taking the stress out of having to know everything from editing to publishing to marketing. This means our authors are free to do what they do best and write. Consequently, we mentor writers through the visioning and goal setting process. Essentially, we help them become authors and achieve a finished manuscript. We work hand-in-hand with our authors, guiding them through the entire process to help them succeed.

We also format finished manuscripts so they're available for readers both physically in bookstores, and on-line for our Kindle readers. Following which, we mentor our authors in the marketing of their published work to reach the widest possible audience.

We recognise that there are a lot of choices out there for publishing services. That's why PCB researched what authors really want and actually need. It's also the reason why we offer a tailored approach.

Our research consistently said that writers *wished they'd had a personal mentor when they first started writing.* Someone who cared and had the expertise to guide them along the path from original idea; to beating the dreaded procrastination, which is really about overcoming limiting self-beliefs and where our writing coaches come in handy; right through to seeing their work in print.

However, the journey doesn't end there as most authors think it does. It's said that *writing a book is the easy part; it's the marketing of it when the real work starts.* That's why PCB also helps its authors stand out in a crowded market place with a marketing strategy to reach the widest possible audience and achieve maximum sales.

Our expertise enables us to provide support to new writers going through every tough spot imaginable, to just being there for the more experienced authors.

www.PenCraftBooks.com

Made in the USA
Monee, IL
07 July 2026

56552040R00079